# GOD'S COUNSEL
## ON MARRIAGE & PARENTING

**By David Meengs**

**God's Counsel on Marriage and Parenting**
By David Meengs
English

Copyright 2013
© Biblical Counseling Trust of India

All Scripture quotations are from the New International Version unless otherwise mentioned.

Published and distributed by Biblical Counselling Trust of India
Plot No. 1, Muthu Mari Amman Koil Street,
Madhavaram, Chennai – 600 060, South India.

E-mail: bcworldwide@hotmail.com


ISBN : 978-0-9849619-2-4

Cover photo courtesy of J.B. Johnson Photography
Printed by Dickinson Press Inc.

Dedicated to the one I love,

My wife, Mary

# Acknowledgments

We are first of all thankful to our God for giving us the Bible, our guide for marriage and life. Without the knowledge of God's Word, what we write would only be our opinion.

I also want to thank my wife for being an excellent Biblical model of a helper. In addition to the many "normal" household duties and the raising of four children, she has patiently spent many hours on the computer making corrections. Because of her, this book is much more readable.

Also, thanks to the staff at the Biblical Counselling Trust of India for their many efforts to bring this book and many other documents to the people of India and other parts of the world.

David Meengs

# Contents

## Part 1 – Marriage God's Way

# Part 2 – Parenting God's Way

# Introduction to Marriage

God arranged the first marriage, and it was a love marriage. A love marriage according to the Bible is not when the boy or the girl decides whom they will marry. That is what happens in the cinema as the boy gets the girl, and the girl gets the boy. Such a practice has more to do with lust than love. A Biblical love marriage is a lifetime, covenantal, sacrificial, commitment of one, not so perfect man and one, not so perfect woman. Commitment is the cause of love, not the other way around. A Biblical love marriage sacrificially gives to the spouse even when there is a lack of money, lack of health, and there are many family problems. A Biblical love marriage doesn't give up when the spouse sins.

A love marriage in the world's eyes is mostly about physical attraction. It is true, we must be attracted to our spouses! But, the problem with putting the physical part first is: what will you do when your husband or wife is 30 kilo's more and there are lots of wrinkles? Will you secretly or openly want another partner in life? If that is so, then you do not have a love marriage. We are not suggesting that all arranged marriages are correct either. God has rules for the selection of a spouse that we will discuss. There is much argument and confusion concerning these things. We need to know the mind of God concerning marriage.

Marriage is not of human origin. Jesus said God is the One who made man, who made the woman, and who put them together (Matthew 19:4-5). It was God who first used the words marriage, husband, wife, bridegroom and bride. It was sinful man who distorted the beauty and good theology, in the meaning of these words. Understanding these words and putting them into practice will build a Biblical marriage and honor God.

In the face of all the evil around us, a Biblical marriage is still the foundational relationship that builds a sound society. In fact, marriage is even the smallest subunit of the Church, because a Biblical husband and wife is a picture of Christ and the Church.

However, as we look around, we see broken and troubled marriages. We see problems like anger, adultery, drunkenness, fear, worry, and depression that are making marriages miserable. But, we can have hope! The pain and misery of these problems can be overcome, if we follow God's prescribed methods. God is still the Wonderful Counselor, and the Prince of Peace. God through Christ continues to heal people spiritually and physically. The Church is commanded to lead the way in the healing process. We write these few chapters to shine the light of the Word, directly on the problems in marriage.

Today our marriages are under attack by the lies of the world that say personal pleasure and personal satisfaction is the main goal in life. The insane search for such personal and selfish goals, along with the primary approval from people outside the marriage, is the undoing of the peace and contentment that only God can give. Selfish love embraces the lies of Satan and destroys the institution of marriage. Selfish love promotes living two separate lives. The Bible does say, *"in the last days men will be lovers of themselves,"* 2 Timothy 3:1b-2a. Biblical love in marriage promotes a oneness with God, the man, and the woman.

God's ideas on how to live are so different from how we as sinful people want to live. It should not come as a surprise then, that God's Word and ways do not follow a single culture in the world. Indeed, the Word of God cuts away at the traditions of men, which really is what culture is all about. Be prepared then, for the double-edged sword of God, His Word. It cuts us and it hurts, and it should.

In stating God's purposes in this marriage discussion, we will be quick and to the point. It is not the will of God or ours to waste your time with endless talk and sugarcoat the problems. We will speak the truth with love, plainly, even if it hurts.

However, another warning is needed for all of us, myself included! Talk in itself does not change people! Sinful habits need to be replaced with changed living. If Biblical truth is read but not applied, it is of no value to the reader. James says, *"Do not merely listen to the Word, and so deceive yourselves. Do what it says,"* James 1:22. Blessings in the Christian life are conditional to our obedience or being faithful in living God's way. It is never easy to change. We need to confront our failures, confess them, receive forgiveness from God and others, and then, with a plan, follow the right path.

All churches should develop and require counseling sessions prior to marriage! Then, many future problems would be headed off before they begin. Scripture says, *"All hard work brings a profit, but mere talk leads only to poverty"* Proverbs 14:23. How much more this is true concerning the Word of God. Thus it will take some effort to look up verses and meditate on God's wisdom. May we not be so busy chasing less important tasks, than improving our marriages. May we not wait until we feel like it, as the evil one will make sure the feeling never comes. We must be a blessing to our spouse, and in the end, promote the kingdom of God!

**David Meengs**

9

# Chapter 1

# A Biblical Husband and Wife

### What is a bridegroom and husband?

Bridegroom is the Biblical name given to a new husband. As the name suggests, it is his responsibility to groom the bride. A Christian man grooms himself and his wife by cleaning up the body and soul, and presenting it to God and the world as holy and acceptable (Rom1 2:1).

The command for a husband to groom a wife is clear. *"Husbands, love your wives, just as Christ loved the church and gave Himself for her,"* Ephesians 5:25. Christ loved the Church to *"present it to Himself as a radiant church, without stain or wrinkle or any other blemish,"* Ephesians 5:27a. Christ did not find the Church lovely. Remember, the Church is the people not the building. He made the Church lovely as He gave Himself graciously for it!  Graciously cared for, a well-groomed bride will blossom like a fragrant flower.

A husband grooming his bride notices every little detail about her, since he must closely inspect her for the purpose of making her more beautiful. Husbands are to be like Christ who makes the Church, (us redeemed sinners) more beautiful by His close attention to us. As a husband grooms his bride, she is made lovelier.

A married man is called a husband. The meaning is significant. Husband is part of the word husbandry, which is the meticulous care of a vineyard, trees, plants, or animals.  Likewise, a husband by God's definition is also involved in the meticulous care of a wife. Husbandry was a foundational task or job God gave to Adam and also for farmers today. *"The Lord God took the man and put him in the Garden of Eden to work it and take care of it,"* Genesis 2:15.

Marriage then is also a responsibility to groom. Bride and groom are simply two words that mean exactly what they say. Any man who is faithful in husbandry or farming will have beautiful gardens and healthy crops. Any man who is faithful in grooming his wife will have a beautiful wife.

11

**Neglect in grooming brings weeds and problems.**

Any farmer or gardener knows that if a field is neglected, weeds will naturally grow. All crops suffer from the lack of nutrition and care. The result is always the same, wilted and diseased plants due to unhealthy growing conditions. It is not very profitable to farm this way. A husband who ignores his wife will have the same condition as a field that is ignored. It will be an unprofitable venture. The wife and children will suffer, just as crops suffer from the lack of care.

**Water is needed for husbands and wives to be healthy.**

Crops and animals need lots of water to be well nourished. We need lots of water also! It is the husband's responsibility as the head of the home to be, *"washing with water through the Word,"* Ephesians 5:26. This means it is the husband's responsibility to make sure that the Bible is read in the home. Why? Because it is the Word of God that changes the hearts of people. When hearts change, thoughts, words and actions will change. When thoughts, words and actions change, emotions/feelings will change. When emotions change, the wife blooms like a beautiful flower. The big question is: Are we reading the Word in the home or are we foolishly, "too busy"?

**Beauty comes from a changed heart.**

When a wife's heart is transformed by the Spirit of God, and softened by the love of her husband, her whole countenance will glow so that she is outwardly beautiful also. A wife with a soft, gentle heart on the inside will reflect and radiate that love on the outside. The two go together, and the bridegroom or husband is responsible for these things. He is the husbandman. If the wife is not more beautiful after years of marriage, the husband should not complain. He is the groom.

We have a beautiful, caring God who designed very simple words to show the responsibilities husbands have for their wives and families. Wives need to know this is the husband's responsibility! Wives must encourage, not criticize. Many husbands have given up, because the wives do not encourage them to lead the home spiritually.

## What is a bride?

A woman first becomes a bride on the day of her marriage, although the preparation takes much time. A bride is described in the Bible as one who *"has made herself ready,"* Revelation 19:7b, for the bridegroom. *"Ready"* carries the meaning of having "made herself right" for her husband. She is dressed in *"fine linen, bright and clean,"* Revelation 19:8. *"Fine linen,"* carries the meaning of a righteous act in Isaiah 61:10. This one woman is the *"right"* one for this one man. Also, *"a bride adorns herself with her jewels,"* Isaiah 61:10. A Christian bride intends to sparkle for her husband and be a jewel in his crown. In the very same way, as Christians, we are jewels to God. The Church is the bride of Christ reflecting the close relationship that the bride must have to the bridegroom.

## What is a wife?

Quite simply, a married woman is a wife. In Scripture, a wife is described as *"a helper,"* Genesis 2:18 & 20, *"her husband's crown,"* Proverbs 12:4b, *"a good thing,"* Proverbs 18:22, and *"your partner,"* in Malachi 2:14. These words are instructive for us all.

A Biblical wife is described in Proverbs 31 as one with virtue. Her husband has full confidence in her in vs. 11. *"She brings him good, not harm, all the days of her life,"* in vs. 12. She *"works with willing hands,"* in vs. 13. She *"brings her food,"* in vs. 14 NKJV. She has a small business outside the home in vs. 16. She gives to the poor in vs. 20. She manages the household in vs. 27. She is praised by her children and husband in vs. 28. She is *"a woman who fears the Lord,"* vs. 30, and is praised for her work by many in vs. 31. She is a beautiful helper, deeply appreciated by her family!

## Christian women grow more beautiful!

A Christian wife is a beautiful woman who will continue to grow in her beauty. A Christian woman will always be more beautiful than the women of the world because real beauty radiates from a heart softened by the Word and Spirit of God. In other words, a heart that is soft and gentle on the inside has the effect of changing the outward

13

features and complexion of the woman also. A smiling heart soon becomes a smiling face!

### Worldly women will lose their beauty!

A woman of the world attempts to make up for a lack of real beauty on the inside by adding paint and ornaments to the outside. God hates external beauty in a woman if inward beauty is not present (Isaiah 3:16-17)! God even vows to remove the external beauty from a woman who is internally ugly, (Isaiah 3:18-24). After ten verses of how God will take outward beauty away, a worldly woman *"shall lament and mourn and she being desolate shall sit on the ground,"* Isaiah 3:26b NKJV.

### A Biblical wife is a companion.

In the creation process, a bride and a wife came into the picture because man was lonely. Adam did not yet have a companion suitable for him. A wife was the part of man that was missing early in the Genesis account and so it is today. A wife is lovingly referred to as a man's better half, but "other half" would be more Biblical. A Biblical wife truly does complete a man!

### A Biblical wife is a submissive wife.

Many "liberated" women are leaving the husband and family to find their fulfillment in the world. But the very approval, peace, and satisfaction they are looking for will not be found! Only God can give this fulfillment in the role He provided for women. Unless a woman has the gift of singleness, she finds fulfillment by being a godly wife and mother in a covenant of companionship - marriage.

### God is the main cure for loneliness, not marriage.

Many enter into a marriage because they are lonely. Even though loneliness is one of the reasons for getting married, a union to Christ is the only permanent cure for loneliness. Without Christ, a person who marries to cure their loneliness problem, will face the reality that they are still lonely. Every human life is created with a spiritual need that only the Spirit of God can satisfy. The rich are as lonely as the poor! Money never satisfies the need of the soul to be loved! God is love and He has the power to put His love in us.

*"Look at the birds of the air; they do not sow or reap or stow away in barns, yet your heavenly Father feeds them. Are you not much more valuable than they?"* Matthew 6:26.

If God knows intimately the animals, the birds, and even plants, how much more He cares about every hurt and pain we have. So, seek not to get from a spouse what only God can give. Filled with God's love, we are able to love. It is only when we have a solid relationship with God that we are able to have a stable relationship with a husband or wife.

# Chapter 2

# Foundational Marriage Truths

Most of the foundational truths for marriage are set forth in Genesis. We read that the Triune God created the world in five days. Then on the sixth day God created various animals and man. God created male and female animals so that they could be fruitful and multiply. *"But for Adam no suitable helper was found,"* Genesis 2:20b. Man's lifetime helper was not an animal, as the animal was not *"suitable"* for man. That is why God created the woman because man needed her help! *"Then the Lord God made a woman from the rib He had taken out of the man, and He brought her to the man,"* Genesis 2:22.

Matthew Henry has a beautiful quote concerning God taking woman from the rib of man:

> "The woman was *'made out of a rib out of the side of Adam.'* She was not made out of his head to rule over him, nor out of his feet to be trampled on by him, but out of his side to be equal with him, under the arm to be protected, and near his heart to be beloved."

It is important to note that God did not make "women" (plural) for man, but He made a woman for a man. This rules out polygamy. God did not make a man for a man, or a woman for a woman, ruling out homosexuality. In Genesis 3:20, Adam called his wife "Eve" not "Steve." Today, we need to know that these rules are God's rules and His design.

### There are differences between a man and a woman.

There is a God-designed difference between a man and a woman. If we do not understand these differences and keep them in mind, there will soon be marriage problems.

**Man was created to perform a task.**

When God created man (Adam), He gave him a job or task to do. It is recorded in Genesis 2:19-20. The task was to name the animals and manage God's creation. After sin entered the world, God reduced man from a manager to a laborer. The task became much harder by God's design.

> *"Cursed is the ground because of you; through painful toil you will eat of it all the days of your life. It will produce thorns and thistles for you, and you will eat the plants of the field. By the sweat of your brow you will eat your food,"* Genesis 3:17b-19a.

**Woman was then created to be a helper to the task.**

Then God said, *"But for Adam no suitable helper was found,"* Genesis 2:20b. Animals were created already and were not to be the primary helper for man. *"Neither was man created for the woman, but woman for the man,"* 1 Corinthians 11:9. After the fall, after sin came into the world, the woman's difficulties in being a helper increased. Because the woman fell into sin first, God said to her, *"your desire will be for your husband,"* Genesis 3:16b. Thus by created design and as part of the curse after the fall, a woman desires and craves a close relationship with her husband, making a woman very relationship-oriented.

These differences are very important to note for the smooth running of a marriage. It is right here that problems come for not observing the God-given roles of men and women. We will see how the problems develop.

**A man can be too focused on the task!**

When a man first courts or seeks a wife, he most often spends much time winning her confidence in him. She interprets all this attention as, "He is really interested in relationships, just like me." She doesn't completely understand that the getting of a wife is his current "task or job." Soon after they are married, she finds him mostly working, leaving little time for her. Since she is very interested in relationships, she is upset and confused and then bitterness easily sets in. If the

18

husband is too intent on his task and does not meet this wife's deep relational needs, it will be much easier for her to be unfaithful to her husband.

It is also quite wrong and even sinful then, when some husbands have a more meaningful relationship with the family dog or the cows they use to plow with. They can talk to the animals much of the day, only to come into the house and say almost nothing to their wives! The Bible reminds a husband to take care of the primary relationship, the wife. "*She is your partner, the wife of your marriage covenant*" Malachi 2:14b. If a husband does not fulfill his proper role in the marriage, mainly giving a real relationship, he actually presents a big "temptation" for his wife to sin and be unfaithful. She is wrong if she does. But the husband in not innocent since he is responsible to give that relationship.

### A wife can also be too focused on other relationships!

When the woman is first interested in the man, she may polish his motorbike, talk about cricket or football, and ask many questions about his work life. The man interprets this attention with great delight! He actually thinks that this woman is interested in his various tasks! But then, soon after marriage, the husband cannot understand it when his wife is more interested in spending time with her family and what they are doing, than in his God-given task. It is wrong for her to spend more time pursuing relationships with her family and friends and encouraging what they are involved in than in encouraging her own husband.

A Biblical wife is also more interested in her husband's task than her children's task! It is such a temptation for the wife and mother to get so wrapped up in the children's activities that she literally ignores the husband. Even if the husband does not take much of an interest in the children's activities she is wrong to ignore her husband and his needs. She needs to remember that God's way of dealing with difficulties is to overcome evil with good. God created her out of a man to be part of a man. She is to be "*a helper suitable for him,*"

Genesis 2:18b. And, *"your desire will be for your husband,"* Genesis 3:16b. She must be adorned for her husband first.

### What can be done if both spouses are wrong?

Both spouses need to change their expectations and meet the other's needs. The man needs to spend less time rubbing and shining his water buffalo or motorbike, and more time rubbing and shining his wife spiritually, emotionally, physically, and intellectually. Finally, God put a man and woman in the Garden of Eden, not a parent and child, not a man and a dog.

### What about paying a dowry to obtain a husband/wife?

In the Bible, dowry was a sum of money or goods a man paid as proof that he was able to support a wife and was also insurance in case he didn't. In the Old Testament, a dowry price secured a woman as a wife. The money was paid to her parents to be held as a guaranteed protection package in case of desertion or divorce. Without the customary bride price of a dowry, the woman in the Bible was simply a concubine or a mistress.

If a man caused a woman to lose her virginity, he had to pay the highest bride price of 50 shekels of silver as a penalty. Fifty shekels today would cost 3 lacks of Rupees or $6400. The dowry price was negotiable in most cases. Saul required David to pay a dowry of 100 lives from the enemies of Saul. But then, Saul really wanted David dead.

### Examples of dowry in the Bible.

We read about dowries in Genesis 34, Exodus 22:16-17, Deuteronomy 2: 28, 29, and Exodus 21:7-11. There was one case in Joshua 15:16-19, where the father of the bride (Caleb) paid a gift to his daughter. In the Bible, the money did not go to either of the parents for their use or expenses. The dowry was required in covenant Christian homes because of so much cheating and stealing. Again, the purpose of the dowry was to protect the bride.

An unbiblical dowry leaves the woman in a serious position if the man finds no pleasure in her, as was the case in Deuteronomy 24:1.

We do not find any example of dowry in the New Testament. Today, dowries too often look more like an old age pension plan for either the parents of a boy or girl, depending on the country.

## What about crossing caste to marry?

The Bible does not prohibit marrying out of caste. In fact, *"Miriam and Aaron spoke against Moses because of the Ethiopian woman whom he had married; for he had married an Ethiopian woman,"* Numbers 12:1 NKJV. Twice in the same verse, God points out that Moses married out of caste. God was angry with Miriam and Aaron because they were speaking against God's servant, Moses! As punishment, *"suddenly Miriam became leprous, as white as snow,"* Numbers 12:10b NKJV. God severely disciplined the sister of Moses, partly because she and Aaron spoke evil of their brother's out of caste marriage. Granted, Moses being righteous was also an issue.

More examples of marrying out of caste were: Abraham in Genesis 16:1, Joseph in Genesis 41:45, Ruth and Boaz, Salmon & Rahab, David in 1 Samuel 18:27, and many others. In fact, Jesus' physical heritage is a result of crossing castes, all for our benefit and understanding.

God looks at the hearts of people, and so should we. Jesus was the King of heaven and He crossed all caste as He touched lepers, prostitutes, the blind and the lame. Christ, as the bridegroom, married the bride (redeemed sinners) *"from every tribe and language and people and nation,"* Revelation 5:9. Furthermore, God adopted them all as sons and daughters in Christ.

Men or women do not sin when they marry out of caste, nor do they sin when they marry in caste. The rule that you must marry in caste only, is partly an invention of man (in every country) to keep the power and wealth in the hands of a few. Jesus said, *"How hard it is for the rich to enter the kingdom of God,"* Mark 10:23.

In Christ, we are all sons and daughters of God and there is neither slave nor free for all are one in Christ (Galatians 3:26-29). Each must marry in the Lord, according to the will of the Lord.

# Chapter 3

# Biblical Reasons for Marriage

**The Bible gives at least three good reasons for marriage:**
- A Biblical marriage gives helpful companionship.
- A Biblical marriage produces godly children.
- A Biblical marriage is given to avoid sexual immorality.

## 1. A Biblical marriage gives helpful companionship.

"It is not good for the man to be alone; I will make a helper suitable for him" Genesis 2:18b. God gives us a good explanation of just what it means to be a "suitable" helper or in the NKJV a "comparable helper." Suitable companions in the Bible are marriage partners who are equally yoked. "Do not be yoked together with unbelievers. For what do righteousness and wickedness have in common? Or what fellowship can light have with darkness?" 2 Corinthians 6:14. We have clear words on how a man and a woman are to be one. God also gives us a picture of being "yoked," as two oxen or horses, working together to accomplish God's design for life. There are 3 Biblical requirements to be equally yoked.

**A. Both must be Christians.** They must share the same faith! Both must be completely committed to Christ. Being "in Christ" is a necessity to have a mature marriage. For our discussion here, we will separate levels of spiritual maturity.

**A nominal Christian** – is a man or woman who goes to church but is not committed to Christ. A pharisee was a nominal Christian. A nominal Christian pretends to be for Jesus in the church on Sunday, but is all for themselves the rest of the week. A nominal Christian looks good on the outside but the heart is unchanged by the Word and Spirit of God. Jesus called a nominal Christian a whitewashed tomb. A nominal Christian is self-righteous, angry, bitter, unforgiving, and not interested in personal Bible study, personal prayer, or

23

increasing obedience to the Word of God. A nominal Christian is a "pretending Christian."

Nominal Christians are more repulsive to God than unbelieving pagans. Jesus said about "nominal Christians, *"I know your deeds, that you are neither cold nor hot. I wish you were either one or the other! So, because you are lukewarm – neither hot nor cold – I am about to spit you out of my mouth,"* Revelation 3:15-16. Beware, churches have "nominal Christians"! A nominal Christian as a potential marriage partner is completely outside the will of God.

**A baby Christian -** is actually much different from a nominal Christian. A baby Christian will surely continue to change for good the rest of their life because Christ is in their heart! With a changed heart, a baby Christian is beginning to walk God's way in life; is interested in prayer; is interested in Bible study. The big difference between a nominal Christian and a baby Christian is that God's grace is in them for the rest of their life. We need this grace in our marriage or we will have problems! See some of the benefits God gives a baby Christian:

> *"My sheep listen to my voice; I know them, and they follow Me. I give them eternal life, and they shall never perish; no one can snatch them out of my hand,"* John 10:27-28. Paul said, *"God's gifts and His call are irrevocable,"* Romans 11:29. Also, *"being confident of this, that He who began a good work in you will carry it on to completion until the day of Christ Jesus,"* Philippians 1:6.

The easiest way to see the difference between a nominal Christian and a baby Christian is not how they live on Sunday, but how they live the other six days of the week! The difference between a baby Christian and a more mature Christian, is that God has been at work changing the mature Christian for a longer period of time.

**An unbeliever –** becoming married to an unbeliever is outside the will of God! An unbeliever will not submit to God or man. Think of the picture God gives us about being equally yoked. Can we yoke a wild ox (unbeliever) and a trained one (Christian)? The wild ox will

24

not even lower it's head so that we can put the yoke on! In the same way, an unbeliever will not humble themselves before God or man and submit to a covenant marriage relationship. If we did manage to get a wild ox in a yoke, how could the plow go forward when the oxen want to go in different directions? A wild ox and a marriage partner are candidates for a yoke, after they are tamed! Don't defile the temple of the living God by being married to an unbeliever!

*"What harmony is there between Christ and Belial? What does a believer have in common with an unbeliever? What agreement is there between the temple of God and idols? For we are the temple of the living God,"* 2 Corinthians 6: 15-16a.

**B. Marriage partners must have a demonstrated desire to solve problems in life God's way, as described in the Bible.** If only one person is committed to solving problems God's way, there will still be a mismatch. A Christian prays to solve problems. A family who prays together stays together. Solving problems requires humility, empathy, and sensitivity to the needs of others. God's way of living demands that the Bible is the only standard for life and conduct. Christian marriages work best when both desire is to live one way, God's way.

**MARRIAGE COMES WITH THIS WARNING:** A beautiful face with an ugly heart will not pull the plow in the direction the Master demands. A beautiful ox with a wild spirit is still wild.

**C. Both spouses must be willing to work.** If a married couple is going to work together like a good team, they must both be willing to pull. A lazy spouse and one with a good work ethic, are not equally yoked. One ox cannot pull the plow if the other is lying down. If you think a spouse who keeps two out of these three points is a good match, talk to someone who has been married for ten years. You are headed for trouble!

**If you think you can change him or her, think again!**

Even though many know these three requirements, they are still thinking, "I know, but I will change him or her." That is really foolish and proud. Only God through the working of His Spirit can change a

25

human heart! Ezekiel 36: 26-38 shows God is in complete control of this salvation and changing process, not us!

Thinking, "I will change him or her," is foolish. People persist in marrying an unbeliever because they are themselves nominal Christians! A Christian follows Christ and the commands of Christ. *"Do not be yoked together with unbelievers,"* 2 Corinthians 6:14a.

### There are examples in Scripture of marriage mismatches.

Abigail was a good woman, married to Nabal whom the Bible calls *"harsh and evil,"* 1 Samuel 25:3 NKJV, and a *"scoundrel"* in verse 25. There are countless marriages today that are filled with heartache, simply because they did not heed God's wise command to be equally yoked. One nominal Christian man complained to his new Christian wife, "This new wedding ring is cutting off my circulation." She reminded him, "It's supposed to!"

### Are two non-Christians equally yoked?

One pastor said he could marry two unbelievers, for they are equally yoked. No way! Try put a yoke on two wild oxen! It will not work until they are first tamed. Can two self-centered people become one when they want to go in different directions? The deeds of the flesh, *"sexual immorality... idolatry... hatred... jealousy, fits of rage, selfish ambition... drunkenness,"* in Galatians 5:19-21, never promote harmony, even if both people are in the midst of them!

One non-Christian woman who finally sought Biblical counsel, said it well. "When I got married I was looking for an ideal, but I got an ordeal, and now I want a new deal." She was not equally yoked!

### 2. A Biblical marriage produces godly children.

One of the primary means God extends His kingdom is by covenantal parents having godly children. God said, *"Be fruitful and increase,"* Genesis 1:28. It is still God's will to have children.

> *"Unless the Lord builds the house, they labor in vain who build it... Children are a heritage from the Lord, the fruit of the womb is His reward... Happy is the man who has his quiver full of them,"* Psalm 127:1, 3, 5a NKJV.

26

First, the Lord must build the family, and they must submit to the Lord. Second, God opens and shuts the womb. Therefore children are *"fruit of the womb, His reward."* Third, happy is the family who has godly children! Not happy is the family who has children. A quiver full of broken arrows is not a blessing to anyone! *"Unless the Lord builds the house, its builders labor in vain"* Psalm 127:1a.

The best way to produce godly children is in a Christian marriage where the spouses are first committed to God, secondly to each other, and thirdly to the children. The order of commitment here is very important to have godly offspring.

## 3. A Biblical marriage was given to avoid sexual immorality.

Christians, *"Do you not know that your bodies are members of Christ Himself?"* 1 Corinthians 6:15a. *"He who unites himself with the Lord is one with Him in spirit,"* 1 Corinthians 6:17. We are made of body and spirit. When we belong to Christ, both our body and spirit belong to Him. God gives us rules for our bodies to obey.

> *"But since there is so much immorality, each man should have his own wife, and each woman her own husband,"* 1 Corinthians 7:2. *"Flee from sexual immorality,"* 1 Corinthians 6:18a.

We don't get married just to flee sexual immorality! But it is one of the reasons God gives to get married. God gave the man and woman a desire for sexual relations. It is a good gift, as all gifts from God are good. However, God regulates the use of this gift to marriage alone if the qualifications mentioned earlier about being equally yoked are met. Then we have God's blessing to marry.

**"If they cannot control themselves, they should marry. For it is better to marry than to burn with passion," 1 Corinthians 7:9.**

This verse has various implications for marriage. For one, God intends that those who are married should recreate as well as procreate sexually. A husband and wife who are satisfied with the love and affection of each other and God, defeat the lure of the world to pull them away from their spouse and God.

# Chapter 4

# Preparing for Marriage and the Selection of a Spouse

### Preparing for marriage or singleness

First, it must be noted that marriage was the normal design of God for man. God said, *"It is not good for the man to be alone,"* Genesis 2:18a. Therefore, singleness is a special gift. If God calls a Christian to singleness, He will do two things. First, He will equip us with a special service for the church. Second, He will give us the peace and grace to accept it. After Jesus spoke about divorce, His disciples suggested:

> *"'It is better not to marry.' Jesus replied, 'Not everyone can accept this word, but only those to whom it has been given. For some are eunuchs because they were born that way; others were made that way by men; and others have renounced marriage because of the kingdom of heaven. The one who can accept this should accept it,'"* Matthew 19:10b-12.

We need to honor single people whom God has called to service and encourage their gifts! But, whether we seek to be married or to be single, the very same Biblical advice is ours:

1. **Just praying is not enough.**
2. **Discover our gifts.**
3. **Develop our gifts.**
4. **Demonstrate our gifts.**
5. **Let God decide.**

### 1. Just praying is not enough.

"Just pray and God will send a husband or wife" is partially true, but greatly flawed! It is when we are actively engaged in doing the Lord's work (even in arranged marriages) that other committed Christians will recognize our gifts and prayerfully consider how we

29

might be a good match for someone they know. Simply waiting in a closed room praying for marriage is as silly as praying, "Give me this day my daily bread" and then going back to bed. God wants to give us daily bread, but we need to go to work. *"If a man will not work, he shall not eat,"* 2 Thessalonians 3:10. If we seek a spouse, go to work! Many people are not eating of the delights of marriage because they are not going to work!

## 2. Discover our gifts.

After conversion, God by the working of the Holy Spirit gives each Christian at least one gift, *"to prepare God's people for works of service,"* Ephesians 4:12a. *"We have different gifts, according to the grace given us,"* Romans 12:6a. In Romans 12:6b-8, 1 Corinthians 12: 8-10, and Ephesians 4:11, some of the various gifts are listed. The different spiritual gifts are *"to serve others,"* 1 Peter 4:10. God called us to Christ to serve the body of Christ. The only condition necessary to serve others with our life is dying to self first - a most difficult task. It is only when we stop loving self first and begin to serve others that we will even know our gifts. Why? Because then others, in thanksgiving, will tell us just how we have been a blessing in their lives. We must start serving with our life and discover our gifts. When people both see men and women serving others, they will then know that we will make a good spouse!

## 3. Develop our gifts.

Building God's church and edifying others is the Christian life. We must schedule our time to help others whether it is teaching, serving, contributing, leadership, administrative, etc.... (Romans 12:7,8). Remember, *"we are God's workmanship, created in Christ Jesus to do good works, which God prepared in advance for us to do,"* Ephesians 2:10. Glorify God by valuing and developing the gift or gifts God has given us. When single people develop their gifts, they are other-oriented for God's glory and for the well-being of mankind. That is what the loving Ten Commandments teach us.

### 4. Demonstrate our gifts.

As we lovingly demonstrating our gifts as service to God and are a blessing to others, God's church is being built. It is then that other men or women will see not only our good service, but also our preparation, and readiness for marriage. There is a cute saying: "Beauty is only skin deep, but character goes to the bone." This is not to say that physical appearance like cleanliness, clothing, hair, weight, are not important to demonstrate, but character or the condition of the heart is most important. These are all part of Christ cleaning up a sinner for His service whether in singleness or marriage. We must make ourself outwardly attractive, but inner attractions are most important! *"Therefore, I urge you, brothers, in view of God's mercy, to offer your bodies as living sacrifices, holy and pleasing to God — this is your spiritual act of worship,"* Romans 12:1.

### 5. Let God decide.

God knows whether we are to do our task in life alone or with a helper. God knows the conditions for His church and how He has prepared us to serve it. Ask God about it openly! He is our father. We can't expect God to lead us tomorrow to a spouse if we are not willing to follow Him today!

**Summary:** So many people today are crying out to God for a special revelation to show them a husband or wife. They are literally lying down, face up, looking for God, still in bed, crazy and lazy! We must pray and then get busy. A shepherd (Jesus) never leads sheep that are standing still! It is in the living and doing of the normal events of life that God will adjust the people and situations for His glory and our good, including the marriage relationship. But don't forget to work on our relationship with our God. We need to be right with God, before we can be right for others. The Good Shepherd is busy gathering in sheep, (not sheep and goats). He will direct us to the person (sheep) of His choice unless He gives us the gift of singleness.

### The selection process of a spouse

In the selection process, there is often a lot of conflict between a young man or woman and their parents. How involved should each one be in the marriage arrangement? The Bible does have something to say on the subject of making decisions. There are also examples in Scripture. First of all, there is a difference between a young lady and a young man in the forming of a new marriage. A *"man will leave his father and mother and be united to his wife,"* Genesis 2:24. So the man leaves his home when he is married. Then we can see that the woman is given in marriage. After God made the woman, *"He brought her to the man,"* Genesis 2:22b.

In Numbers 30 we see more of God's wisdom on making decisions in the home including the selection of a spouse. Even though all the verses are important, we will concentrate on just a few.

> *"When a young woman still living in her father's house makes a vow to the Lord or obligates herself by a pledge and her father hears about her vow or pledge but says nothing to her, then all her vows and every pledge by which she obligated herself will stand. But if her father forbids her when he hears about it, none of her vows or the pledges by which she obligated herself will stand; the Lord will release her because her father has forbidden her,"* Numbers 30:3-5.

Here we see how the father as the head of the home is responsible for the final decision. However, he is a foolish man if his wife and child are not involved in the decision making process. *"Where there is no counsel, the people fall; but in the multitude of counselors there is safety,"* Proverbs 11:14 NKJV.

God also speaks clearly about when the man of the house (husband) fails to make a decision because the wife or other family member has his/her own idea about something.

> *"If she marries after she makes a vow or after her lips utter a rash promise by which she obligates herself and her husband hears about it but says nothing to her, then her vows or the*

*pledges by which she obligated herself will stand. But if her husband forbids her when he hears about it, he nullifies the vow that obligates herself, or the rash promise by which she obligates herself, and the Lord will release her,"* Numbers 30:6-8.

If a wife and daughter agree to a marriage proposal and the husband/father is aware but does not speak, he affirms their decision even in his silence. He cannot at a later date blame the daughter or wife of making a poor decision. He agreed to it when he did not object. Read all of Numbers 30 for a more full explanation.

### The dating game is dangerous.

Young people need to be very careful. The whole scene of recreational dating is dangerous (Genesis 34:1-2). Being alone with a member of the opposite sex is filled with temptation. The greatest danger is that the young man or woman can fall in love quickly. God's process is not to first fall in love and then consider if he or she is the right person. No, God's ways are to consider the godly qualifications, and then fall in love. The dating scene is too often filled with falling in love before the qualifications are considered.

In the end, a married man and woman are called to love each other both body and soul. So they do need to be physically and spiritually attracted to each other! God says, the soul must be your first concern and not appearance, skin color, education, or money.

I think we all would agree that it is easy to see if a person is attractive outwardly. But the matters of the heart is what really makes the person. So take the time to find out before you fall in love, before you are married. Besides, love at first sight is usually falling in lust anyway, which we will discuss in the sixth chapter.

### Supervised group social encounters

The church needs to do a much better job of having regular meetings for the youth with the dual purpose of serious spiritual training, and for social interaction. I know of ladies who are in their 40's and want to be married. They do not have Christian relatives or parents to help them. The church needs to get involved for the right reasons- the building of God's kingdom.

When young people and their parents see how the young people react to others, they will learn much about character. So often, very little is known about the real character of a spouse until after marriage. How can two people be equally yoked if nothing is known of the character of a possible spouse? Why is the search for a husband or wife so often in another city or village? Are too many people in your own place aware of the character flaws of the one you are trying to get married? There is so much lying and pretending going on in the whole selection process and it needs to stop! It is sinful! Talk openly about faults and limitations. If someone sold you a sick animal as a healthy one, would you not feel cheated? How much worse it is to lie and pretend you are better than you really are just to secure a marriage to the one you pretend to love!

**Two common mistakes happen in the selection of a spouse.**

First, the parents choose without consulting their child. Wise parents discuss marriage openly and involve the children in the process. In fact, part of the process of letting go of the children, is the parents working with them in the selection of a future partner in life. If children are old enough to marry, they are also old enough to help decide whom to marry. After all, they need to live with the decision the rest of their lives.

Second, some children do not involve the parents or other Christians in the marriage selection process. Mature Christians know the joys and difficulties in marriage and can help you be aligned with the will of God in a possible marriage partner. Neither parent nor child should make such an important decision on whom to marry without much prayer and counsel. *"Where there is no counsel, the people fall; but in the multitude of counselors there is safety,"* Proverbs 11:14 NKJV.

**What if a girl is in love with a good Christian man and her parents want her to marry another Christian man?**

If both are really good Christians, then a hurried marriage should not occur. All involved in the decision need to work on changing their own lives (Matthew 7:1-5), pray, and wait for God to make it more clear. God said, *"My ways are higher than your ways,"* Isaiah 55:9b. If we are considering money, looks, and status in society, before looking at the heart like God does we are wrong. Sad to say, so often even Christian parents are too quick to look at status and money. They should know, *"the love of money is a root of all kinds of evil. Some people, eager for money, have wandered from the faith and pierced themselves with many griefs,"* 1 Timothy 6:10. The girl is often too quick to look at appearance. She is reminded,

> *"But the Lord said to Samuel, 'Do not consider his appearance or his height, for I have rejected him. The Lord does not look at the things man looks at. Man looks at the outward appearance, but the Lord looks at the heart,'"* 1 Samuel 16:7.

If all concerned look at the heart, the decision will be in line with God's thoughts. In the end, the Bible is clear. The head of the house is responsible for the final decision. However, the decision must be based on the will of God. The verses above point to that. Also, the order of the Ten Commandments shows that the love and honor of God is before the love and honor of parents. These are difficult issues but not without God's direction.

> *"Do not conform any longer to the pattern of this world, but be transformed by the renewing of your mind. Then you will be able to test and approve what God's will is — His good, pleasing and perfect will,"* Romans 12:2.

# Chapter 5

# Leaving and Cleaving

*"Therefore shall a man leave his father and his mother, and shall cleave unto his wife: and they shall be one flesh,"* **Genesis 2:24 KJV.**

It is because of covenant obligations to God and to the new spouse, that God demands that the new couple leave their parents. The Word of God is clear about where the newlyweds should not live – which is with their parents. Do not think this is "Old Testament" theology. This same verse turns up again in the New Testament.

*"A man shall leave his father and mother and be joined* (cleave) *to his wife, and they shall become one flesh,"* **Matthew 19:5 NKJV.**

God instituted this "leaving" and "cleaving" rule in the Old Testament and Jesus reconfirmed it in the New. The verse begins with a command for the man to *"leave"* his family. The word *"cleave"* in the verse is an old word for the process of the bride and groom coming together to be joined as one. "Cleaving" is more specifically the joining of a man and a woman in marriage spiritually (which includes mentally & emotionally) and physically. The word cleave is not to be used here as cutting with a knife like one confused student thought.

### What does *"leaving"* have to do with covenant?

In the Old Testament, all male children were circumcised the 8th day after they were born. This gave them the sign of the covenant as an initiation rite into the covenant community. At this time the parents in covenant with God, promised to bring up the child in the ways of the Lord. Then when this young boy grew into a man and was ready to be married, he was to "leave" the covenant protection and blessings of his father and family, and begin his own covenant family unit.

The woman or new bride did not really *"leave"* home. Rather her father (and mother) gave her to this man. Thus, the new young bride was never without covenant protection. She transferred from the covenant of her father and family, to enter into a new covenantal union with her husband. This is why many marriage ceremonies today correctly include the pastor asking the parents of the bride, "Who gives this woman to this man?" This question is asked because of covenant obligation and protection.

It was essential that an Israelite woman married a man who had the sign of the covenant which was circumcision, or she was a covenant breaker. In the coming of the Gentile church in the New Testament, baptism took the place of circumcision (Colossians 2:11-13). What was a bloody initiation rite into the covenant became bloodless after Christ shed His blood at the Cross. Today if a man or woman marries someone who is not a baptized member of a Christian church and not a "real" Christian, they are likewise a covenant breaker.

It must be clearly understood that just because someone is born in a Christian family, is baptized, and goes to church, that does not in itself make them a Christian. It is a personal relationship with Jesus Christ alone that makes them a Christian. The Christian "cleaving" of a new couple is only possible after they have first "cleaved" to Christ.

### 1. "Leaving and cleaving" is a command to the parents.

The command to *"leave"* the father and mother means an adult relationship must be established between the parents and their child, replacing the former parent–child relationship. In both the Old and the New Testament God was emphasizing that the new spouse must become the new number one relationship.

#### The parents are commanded to let the children go!

When children are little, parents are supposed to protect and control their children. However, when it is time for the children to *"leave,"* the parents need to grant liberty. God knows a little child that is turning into a man will always be a piece of his/her mother and father. But a husband and wife are to be much closer than just a piece of each other - she is him and he is her. She is his own flesh, and the two are one, that is essentially why a man must *"leave"* and *"cleave."* This is also why adultery is so wrong. If parents hang on to

38

the kids after marriage, God is against them! And don't say it is our culture to hang on to the child. God's Word goes against every culture, because culture is man's way of living.

### Why don't parents tell the truth about not letting go?

The truth is, as parents, we too often have built our lives around our children and we are terrified to see the children leave home, especially the last child. The real problem is there is not a proper relationship between us as husband and wife! If we have not developed a closeness as a husband and wife by this time, shame on us! When parents refuse to let the children *"leave,"* a big problem begins in the new marriage of the children also. Plus, the same problem continues in the older marriage of the parents. Often mummy does not want to lose her boy to another woman, even if it is a new wife.

Her longtime husband shares greatly in the blame! He provoked his wife to get her number one affection from the children because he was "married" to his work, his own mother, or may have an alcohol, gambling, or other problems.

There are other reasons parents don't want to let go of their son or daughter. Parents often have their eye on their children's salary, thinking it would be nice if they could get paid back for their investment in the children's education and marriage. Paul under the inspiration of the Holy Spirit said, *"children should not have to save up for their parents, but parents for their children,"* 2 Corinthians 12:14b.

### Children are getting pulled apart!

The parents are pulling on one arm of their child, and the new spouse pulling on the other in a tug-of-war! The son or daughter is torn apart as to whom he or she must primarily "cleave" to. God has sent every parent a Bible letter that in effect reads: "Parents let go of your son and daughter when they get married so they can cling to their spouse" The new married couple must *"leave"* so they

39

can "*cleave.*" Marriage is such an intimate relationship that one must leave the parents to enter into it.

Parents, even if it's your children that are mainly keeping your marriage together, don't ruin their new marriage by trying to hold on to them. Even a bird with a brain the size of a pea knows enough to push a young bird out of the nest when it is time for the little one to fly on its own.

### How do parents begin to let go of their children?

Parents must begin to let go of the children already when they are little. A small baby does not need to be instantly picked up every time he or she cries. A parent continues to let go when they leave the little baby in the care of family or friends once in a while when they must go away. They let go a little more when the child goes to school by delegating some of the responsibility to the teachers for a certain time. This slowly letting go continues until the child becomes a young man or woman and gets married. In the end, God commands the new married couple to leave so that they can cleave. And parents must let them go!

### 2. "Leaving and cleaving" is a command to a married couple.

The command to "leave" the parents does not suggest that children are to forsake their parents. Scripture is clear that families are to care for their own.

*"If a widow has children or grandchildren, these should learn first of all to put their religion into practice by caring for their own family and so repaying their parents and grandparents, for this is pleasing to God... If anyone does not provide for his relatives, and especially for his immediate family, he has denied the faith and is worse than an unbeliever,"* 1 Timothy 5: 4, 8.

However, the number one relationship for the new husband or wife is still his or her new spouse. The new couple must start their own home as part of their new-shared identity in being joined as one. The new "*cleaving*" of a husband and wife is a picture of the union of Christ and the Church. "*Cleaving*" is necessary in two ways.

40

## Physical "cleaving" is necessary.

A married couple that refuses to be joined as one physically after marriage is against God and their spouse.

*"The wife does not have authority over her own body, but the husband does. And likewise the husband does not have authority over his own body, but the wife does,"* 1 Corinthians 7:4.

God created the man and woman to be more intimate than the rest of creation. All animals were created to procreate (make new life) only. The female animal will usually have nothing to do with the male if it is not for reproductive timings. Sad to say some marriages are even like that. However, God intended for the man and woman to enjoy each other as well as to produce little ones. A man and woman face each other when intimate. Animals do not! Do you see how God intended for the man and woman to enjoy each other in a much deeper relationship than the rest of His creation?

There is nothing unclean about a man and a woman cleaving physically after the marriage ceremony. If it were, then Adam and Eve sinned before they ate from the tree. In fact, it is sinful to deny physical intimacy with your spouse.

In the new marriage relationship, there is much more to the physical oneness than sexual activity. It is important to touch one another lovingly during the day. Sad to say, we can get a better lesson from the animal world than by observing some marriages. Even animals show they like each other's company by how they groom and touch each other, even in public. More than sex was in mind when God said, *"Let the husband render to his wife the affection due her, and likewise also the wife to the husband,"* 1 Corinthians 7:3. *"The affection due"* includes a kind smile, a gentle touch, and a helping hand. These are all very necessary kinds of physical communication that help to build a one-flesh relationship. We are to care for our spouse's physical condition as much we do our own.

**A mental or spiritual "cleaving" is necessary.**

A man and woman also need to be "one flesh" and "cleave" mentally, emotionally, and spiritually. God sees both mental and emotional issues as spiritual ones. Think through this Biblically. "*God will bring every work into judgment, including every secret thing, whether it be good or evil,*" Ecclesiastes 12:14. If God is going to hold us accountable in the Day of Judgment, even for every secret thought, then every mental thought is a spiritual matter. Also, in the New Testament, we are commanded to, "*bring every thought into captivity to the obedience of Christ,*" 2 Corinthians 10:5b.

It is the world, not God, that would have us believe that mental and emotional problems are not a spiritual concern. Some people think becoming spiritually one is when a husband and wife simply go to church on Sunday. If that is the extent of our spiritual oneness as husband and wife we have a covenant with the devil. It is how we think, speak and act all seven days of the week that is our spiritual responsibility.

Today people blame behaviors as "mental problems" to give the suggestion that it is beyond their control to change them. The truth is, "mental hospitals" have taken over much of the work of the church. Worse yet, it was the church and church leaders who even sent the people to the mental institutions, claiming the church did not have the answers for their problems. The Bible is clear in 2 Timothy 3:16-17, and 2 Peter 1:3-4, God has the help that we need.

**Is my particular problem a disease or a spiritual issue?**

Many behavioral issues are also called diseases, instead of sins! For example, take alcoholism. Even the word suggests that it is a disease. The world believes it is. The Bible however calls it by another name, drunkenness. In 1 Corinthians 6 and Galatians 5, we can clearly see that it is a sin. The list only gets larger to include, anger, bitterness, fear, worry and a common result of all these is depression. If these really are diseases, then we should take medication to try to eliminate them! However, we would be much wiser to listen to God and confess

42

our wrong behaviors for what they are: sin, and receive His forgiveness. And then, with a sorrow that leads to repentance, live differently.

There is such a thing as a real "brain injury" as the result of an accident, or a birth defect. But still, there are Biblical principles to guide how a person must act. A Christian husband and wife need to change their personal selfish behavioral habits to become one flesh together, and to be in covenant with God.

### Leaving home spiritually

It is possible for a married person to *"leave"* home in the physical sense but not in a spiritual sense! A new wife has not yet left her father spiritually when she nags her husband, saying, "My father helped my mother buy food and cook." "My father helped with the kids." "My father helped my mother clean the house." My father this, my father that! This wife is still living mentally or spiritually with her father!

The new husband likewise says, "My mother buys good food and cooks so nicely." "My mother knows how to wash clothes better than you." "My mother always has her house clean." This husband is still mentally or spiritually living with his mother! God's command is clear: *"A man will leave his father and mother and be united to his wife, and they will become one flesh,"* Genesis 2:24b.

### Bitter children don't leave their parents either.

A new husband or wife do not leave home "spiritually speaking," if they are bitter or angry towards one or both of their parents. When we are bitter, the very person we are bitter against actually controls us. As a result, we carry them with us wherever we go. Do we have so few responsibilities and relationships in life that we want to carry our parents to dinner, to work, and to bed, all because of our bitterness towards them?

*"If you harbor bitter envy and selfish ambition in your hearts, do not boast about it or deny the truth. Such "wisdom" does not come down from heaven but is earthly, unspiritual, of the devil,"* James 3:14-15.

When we harbor bitterness, happiness will dock elsewhere!

It is a fact, even our families will hurt us. But even then, a mature Christian will confess his or her own sin to God and not dwell on the sin of others! It is so important to work through any bitterness issues because plainly speaking, it is a lack of the forgiveness! The key is, confess the bitterness and replace it with forgiveness (Mark 11:25). Then we will know peace. That in a nutshell is how to come away from bitterness and "cleave," to our spouse and others spiritually.

### Newly married means a new decision unit.

"Leaving and cleaving" spiritually means that the new husband and wife must also become a new decision unit. The parents may give advice, but the new couple must make their own decisions. Right here, we again see the importance of the husband and wife both being real Christians. God says cling to our spouse until death, for he or she is our permanent and primary relationship. Parents and children need to understand these things so that they don't break what God has decreed by covenant.

### God will test you to see if you are "cleaving" spiritually.

How do we react to our spouse's weaknesses? When our spouse is acting in a wrong way, do we respond in anger and lash out at them? Do we respond in bitterness by trying to ignore him or her? Have we been willing to expose their weakness to them alone? Do we somehow withhold our love from our spouse just because they did not love us correctly? If our love to our spouse has been dependent on their love towards us, then we have been manipulative, not interested in grace or cleaving to our spouse in these times.

Jesus said, *"If you love those who love you, what reward will you get,"* Matthew 5:46a? The scolding of our spouse for his or her wrongs, making their life miserable, is trading *"evil for evil"* according to Romans 12. That, moves us further apart instead of closer to each other.

*"Love is kind,"* and it promotes cleaving and oneness. Being "kind," is even more than being gentle and respectful; it also plans for ways to show love. For example, we must balance gently pointing out our

spouse's faults with compliments for the good things they do! It is common for us to be "very right" in something we say to our spouse, but wrong in how we say it. A wise person once said; "Speaking the truth without love is like doing surgery without anesthesia."

### A counseling example

A man who we recently helped was a good example of pointing out his wife's wrong behavior to the neglect of any compliments for work she did well. The result was a very bitter wife! This proud man refused to work on his own personal, sinful habits and saw only the FAULTS of his wife. He needed to STOP BLAMING HIS SPOUSE for his problems! Granted she had her problems, but for things to change he needed to first see that he was acting like a *"hypocrite,"* Matthew 7:5.

### Jesus is the number one way to oneness with a spouse.

A wall exists in marriage and in life because we are self-centered sinners, born that way. For two people to become closer, just one must be willing to walk with Christ - God's way. Yes, when just one person changes great things begin. It is in Christ, that we break down the wall of separation that exists between God and our spouse. However, for a more complete oneness, two must be willing to deny themselves. Total unity with God and our spouse is the only way to a one-flesh marriage relationship.

In summary, *"She is your companion and your wife by covenant,"* Malachi 2:14b NKJV. Marriage is a "covenant of companionship." *"Therefore shall a man leave his father and his mother, and shall cleave unto his wife: and they shall be one flesh,"* Genesis 2:24.

# Chapter 6

## Lust vs. Love

*"The lust of the flesh, and the lust of the eyes, and the pride of life, is not of the Father, but is of the world,"* 1 John 2:16b NKJV.

We will look at lust versus love in three parts. 1st "The attitude of lust," 2nd "The attitude of love" and 3rd "Moving from lust to love."

### 1. The attitude of lust

Lust covers such a wide range of sinful thoughts, words and actions. Lust is when a man or woman mentally desires or physically touches one who is not their spouse with sexual intent. Simply noticing that a man or woman is attractive is not lust in itself. It is what we do after we notice they are attractive. Dressing provocatively is also lust as it tries to attract others. In almost every country, television, DVD's and the Internet, show scenes that leave little to the imagination as to what the couple (usually not married) is doing, or intends to do. Think through the following series of events to see how subtle lust is.

We watch TV with our friends where two people work their way into bed as we look with great interest. The following day we go to the cinema with our friends. Again two not married, whom we know by name, are intimate on the couch. The next day a friend who is newly married, asks us to watch him and his new wife in the bed, doing what we have been watching on TV, the cinema or on the Internet, or in a magazine. We are shocked by the suggestion! We say, "I would never do that!" But then, we already have watched these things, even with those who are not married. There is a special name called HYPOCRITE for we who would watch something wrong with great delight and then say we would never do it. We have a big problem in our homes and lives called lust! Jesus wants us to understand that anyone who looks lustfully, has already committed adultery. God demands we repent!

Men are not the only ones who lust! Women are increasingly getting bolder, just like the men. For a woman to do what is pictured on television, the movies, and on the Internet, she is really not much of a woman. A real woman is interested in a relationship and a family. A real woman uncovers herself in front of one man, her husband, and not multiple men. Those in the cinema can't give us the close interpersonal relationships that we desire and need. It is Christ first, then family and friends who can bring that fulfillment. But we must change first! The truth is, anyone who is hooked on lust is madly in love with self and wants others to please them! There is something we must know!

**Lust is never satisfied because it always wants more.**

Young teenagers, do you know what you are getting into with this whole lust-pornography scene? Before you jump in so fast, know that lust is never satisfied? More than that, a person enslaved to lust will never be satisfied with God either? *"Don't you know that when you offer yourselves to someone to obey him as slaves, you are slaves to the one that you obey?"* Romans 6:16a. Our eager involvement in the lust scene is a road away from God. Are we so ready to walk away from God at such a young age? The very worst sexual pervert, started with looking at a simple picture of a nude woman! But, he wanted more! Lust starts like a drunkard does, with just one drink!

Did you know, *"Those controlled by the sinful nature cannot please God,"* Romans 8:8? Plus, *"those controlled by the sinful nature,"* cannot please a spouse some day either. Nor can any spouse ever please a person who is enslaved to lust. Not even the most Biblical spouse could satisfy a marriage partner who is selfishly enslaved to lust. The simple reason; "the attitude of lust" is never be satisfied!

A person in lust is like a drug addict who wants a bigger high every time! Lust is like a train without brakes. A sinful man or woman in lust wants what God forbids as their flesh wars against the Spirit of God. Romans 6:13a says: *"Do not offer the parts of your body to sin, as instruments of wickedness, but rather offer yourselves to God."*

Please, I beg you, listen! A real Christian realizes how costly it was for God to shed His Son's blood for our redemption. To sin willfully again and again in lust is to trample the blood of Christ as if it were common blood! A real Christian does not do this! God in love warns us, *"the wrath of God is being revealed from heaven against all the godlessness and wickedness of men who suppress the truth by their wickedness,"* Romans 1:18. God is against us if we want a lust-filled life!

Any person who lustfully rebels, has God's warning! *"Therefore God gave them over in the sinful desires of their hearts to sexual impurity for the degrading of their bodies with one another,"* Romans 1:24. Understand the implications of this warning! God let them continue on the road to hell! It is a fool who would trade a few moments of pleasure for an eternity in hell?

### "The attitude of lust" is idolatry.

This "attitude of lust" always involves bitter envy because it is self-seeking instead of being grateful and thankful. Lustful envy is a *"demonic"* spirit that hates God and a spouse thinking, "You are not giving me what I want or what I deserve." Such a person is an idolater because they think God reports to them! God warns us:

> *"But if you have bitter envy and self-seeking in your hearts, do not boast or lie against the truth. This wisdom does not descend from above, but it is earthly, sensual, demonic,"* James 3:14-15.

### Do you really want to be married to a cinema star?

The world's fickle love (lust) is shown in the cinema as a magic feeling that "just happens." It is not something you work at day by day, nor is it a sacrificial action or about commitment. Cinema people "fall in love," and of course "fall out of love" sooner or later, usually sooner. We need to think through this, because the cinema and movie characters can be so appealing.

Can anyone really find true joy in a movie star that twinkles all over town? Do we really want to be married to someone who is mixed up with other things that lust is associated with like stealing, cheating, lying - all self-centered and associated with adultery? Or, is there joy and satisfaction in being married to someone who is sacrificially devoted to us? Each spouse must be committed to a high standard of morality, and have a steadfast commitment to a holy God and to the other sinful spouse!

### A girl or woman who dresses provocatively is lusting.

Lust is not just a cinema problem. Women dress and walk suggestively for the purpose of attracting male attention, starting at a young age. Clothing styles are getting more revealing, and clothing manufacturers are not the problem! They make what people want!

### Can a man in lust really lead a home?

God calls men to be the head of a home. If a man is involved in lust or pornography, he cannot lead a home. God shows us why: *"I noticed among the young men, a youth who lacked judgment,"* Proverbs 7:7b. Why? He was hooked on a woman *"dressed like a prostitute with crafty intent,"* Proverbs 7:10b. *"With persuasive words she led him astray; she seduced him with her smooth talk. All at once he followed her like an ox going to the slaughter,"* Proverbs 7:21-22a. The underlined words show a man in lust can only follow! A man saying, "It does not matter where I get my appetite, as long as I eat at home," is wrong! God has one word for lust, *"flee,"* 2 Timothy 2:22. Unless this man changes, *"her house is a highway to the grave,"* Proverbs 7:27a.

*"If you live according to the sinful nature, you will die, but if by the Spirit you put to death the misdeeds of the body, you will live,"* Romans 8:13. Flee lust's first beginnings, like you would poison. For the greatest fires begin with just a spark. No momentary pleasure is worth an eternity of torment. Christ changing hearts is the only way to stop this evil scene of lust! God not only teaches us how to say "no" to lust, but how to put on true "love." Sinful life-styles must be replaced!

To put on love, we must pursue righteousness, or the void will once again be filled with lust. We must get a taste of the satisfaction of God's favor, the promises in His Word, His pardon of sin, and His assurance of life and immortality. We must learn to drink the pure living water of love, not the polluted stream of lust. In the next two sections, we will look at how love must be pursued!

## 2. The attitude of love

> *"Love is patient, love is kind. It does not envy, it does not boast, it is not proud. It is not rude, it is not self-seeking, it is not easily angered, it keeps no record of wrongs. Love does not delight in evil but rejoices with the truth. It always protects, always trusts, always hopes, always perseveres. Love never fails,"* 1 Corinthians 13:4-8.

### Love in the Bible is about commitment.

Love in 1 Corinthians 13:4-8 is described as a sacrificial action for another. These verses show us how Biblical love is much more than a changing feeling. When we do these things in the love chapter for another person, we show our love for them. When another person does these things for us, they demonstrate love. Love shows!

Those who are single wait for marriage, to be physically intimate. The reason is, real Biblical love protects the other person from sinning against God and suffering the consequences. There are at least five other reasons underlined in the text above that show why physical intimacy waits for marriage.

### Marriage vows include a commitment to an imperfect spouse.

Love in marriage is an unconditional commitment of body and soul to one person of the opposite sex, an imperfect spouse. That's right. When Christians stand at the altar in God's presence, both are really saying, "I am committed to this sinner for the rest of my life." Then why, when one of the spouses sins, does the commitment to him or her usually falls off? Is that what God does to us when we sin as Christians, or does God love us more by sending His Holy Spirit after us? Look carefully how God models a loving commitment to us:

51

- *"God demonstrates His own love for us in this: While we were still sinners, Christ died for us,"* Romans 5:8.
- *"He who began a good work in you will carry it on to completion,"* Philippians 1:6b.
- *"The Lord will rescue me from every evil attack and will bring me safely to His heavenly kingdom. To Him be glory forever and ever. Amen,"* 2 Timothy 4:18.

We see that the love of God is much more than a feeling! Blessed is the Church's marriage to the Lamb, and blessed is a marriage between a man and a woman that is founded on this kind of sacrificial commitment. Just think! "Will anyone's lust care for another in difficult times? Lust doesn't care for others in good times!

## The most intimate love puts others first.

The most intimate act of love in marriage is that of sacrificially serving the other spouse. Earlier we studied how a woman desires a very close relationship with her husband. This is so true in the marriage bed. A woman often takes longer to have the same pleasure as her husband. He is ready to be intimate when he sees his wife, and can be pleased quickly. She is ready after the husband spends time holding her and some of her emotional/relational needs are met.

The point is: A man with a lust problem is mostly interested in pleasing himself quickly and his wife will be without the same pleasure. That's why being addicted to lust as a youth is so harmful in preparing for marriage! No one can just turn off lust and put on love when they get married. God's wisdom is, *"love is patient,"* 1 Corinthians 13:4. God also said, *"Let the husband render to his wife the affection due her,"* 1 Corinthians 7:3 NKJV. It is so sad that so many men and women have only experienced lust and not love, even in the marriage bed.

## The eyes of love

*"Like a lily among the thorns is my darling among the maidens. Like an apple tree among the trees of the forest is my lover among the young men. I delight to sit in his shade,"* Song of Solomon 2:2-3.

The Song of Solomon is one of the most intimate and beautiful pieces of literature in the world for its accuracy, imagery, moral, and spiritual content. The two verses listed above show how the attitude of love has eyes only for a fiancée or spouse, not others. God in His grace and wisdom gave us the Song of Solomon as part of the Bible. The Song of Solomon is an allegory, which is - a poem, play, or picture, in which the apparent meaning of the characters and events is used to symbolize a spiritual meaning. In other words, the very same words show two pictures. In the first picture, we see the most intimate relationship between Christ and the Church (redeemed sinners). In the second, the same words show the intimacy between a husband and a wife. The Song is so accurate because in Ephesians 5, we see that the relationship of a husband and wife is to be patterned after Christ and the Church.

**The Song of Solomon extols the virtue of love.**

The Song begins with a bride longing for affection. She said, *"Let him kiss me with the kisses of his mouth,"* in Song of Solomon 1:2. This is a picture of the wife longing for affection. The same verse shows how a sinner longs for the affection of Christ. The gospel of grace is the Son embracing us and we embracing the Son.

In 8:1, the bride longs for her husband to be close just as a nursing baby is held close to the mother. Think of how nursing a baby takes much time! A bride also wants to be close for a time and not an instant! Does a sinner only want Christ for an instant? No, we want to be held by Christ and loved for all eternity!

In chapter four, the bridegroom, in the attitude of love, takes time to please and be pleased with all of the bride from head to toe. The bridegroom in love is satisfied with his bride. This is also a picture of the close attention Christ gives to the Church. He can satisfy the needs of even the greatest sinner, and He delights in the relationship. Biblical love, whether it is with a spouse or with Christ, is satisfied. Lust is never pleased with a spouse or the other gods of pornography and sexual impurity.

### Is Christ number one?

When the bride went to the city, she was thinking, "*I will seek the one I love,*" Song of Solomon 3:2b NKJV. She had eyes only for her man! She did not seek out another man or the cinema when she went to the city. Is a relationship to Christ the most important thing in our life? If not, then we are lusting after other gods! In both marriage and with Christ, love is totally satisfied in a sweet relationship, whereas with the various lusts, there will be emptiness. What a difference there is between love and lust!

### Christ and the husband made the bride beautiful.

Note that the brothers of the bride feared they would not find a marriage match for their sister because she lacked breast maturity (8:8). The bride herself said she was not beautiful when the bridegroom first met her. Her own words, "*I am a wall*" in 8:10, showed she lacked a womanly figure. But then, the husband made her beautiful! Listen to her words, "*Then I became in his eyes as one who found peace,*" 8:10b, NKJV. Do not think that this is overstating the situation. In 1:6, the bride admitted, "*Do not stare at me because I am dark… My mother's sons were angry with me and made me take care of the vineyards; my own vineyard I have neglected.*"

Think about the double meaning here. We are dark sinners, neither beautiful nor mature. We can only agree with Isaiah, "*Woe is me, for I am undone,*" Isaiah 6:5a NKJV! In our lost condition, Christ transforms us from dark sinners to beautiful redeemed saints! How Christ cleans up a sinner by His grace is more than a suggestion for husbands. Christ presented a glorious Church to Himself. He did not find the Church beautiful! He made her beautiful by His sacrificial actions!

**Young men and husbands**, you will someday be a **bridegroom** or you already are one. Never forget, it is our life long responsibility to do as the word suggests—groom the bride. It is a word that God made, filled with meaning for us! However, until we can say, "*Like a lily among the thorns is my darling among the maidens,*" Song of Solomon 2:2, we do not have the eyes of love! Like "*lilies among* *thorns*" is exactly how Christ sees His redeemed sinners. Tragically, the eyes of lust sees a wife as a thorn and all other ladies as lilies! This is an accurate picture of the difference between lust and love.

**Ladies,** the next verse is for you. *"Like an apple tree among the trees of the forest is my lover among the young men. I delight to sit in his shade."* Can you truly say this about your husband or husband to be? Or would you rather be in the shade of (close to) another? If you delight to be in the company of another man more than your husband, even though not for sex, you are still in a lustful and adulterous situation.

We must be also interested in Christ alone as our God or we have a spiritual adultery problem! How blessed is our relationship to the Lamb! How blessed is the pure relationship of a husband and wife! God's commands concerning love verses lust have the highest logic, and obedience to them, the greatest sweetness! What peace we have when we are doers of the Word and not hearers only!

### But my cold spouse is to blame for my lustful thinking.

If we think others are the main reason we do wrong things we need to hear Jesus words. *"You hypocrite, first take the plank out of your own eye, and then you will see clearly to remove the speck from your brother's eye,"* Matthew 7:5. Real Biblical repentance begins with this verse in Matthew 7:5. When one spouse is committed to changing his/her own life, a healing of a relationship begins.

We must never blame God for our lust problems either. Nor should we think God is going to solve them for us. God clearly showed us that repentance is our problem to correct. To Cain He said, *"If you do what is right, will you not be accepted? But if you do not do what is right, sin is crouching at your door; it desires to have you, but you must master it,"* Genesis 4:7. We are responsible to repent. God will give us the strength if we will but ask for it. Cain didn't change and he was cast out from the presence of God and became a wanderer. Will we wander and repeat his folly, or humble ourselves, pray, repent, and begin to love God and others?

The 3rd part, moving from lust to love, is the next chapter.

# Chapter 7

# Moving from Lust to Love

The following verses clearly show us the importance of moving from lust to love.

*"It is God's will that you should be sanctified: That you should avoid sexual immorality; that each of you should learn to control his own body in a way that is holy and honorable, not in passionate lust like the heathen, who do not know God; and that in this matter no one should wrong his brother (or sister) or take advantage of him. The Lord will punish men for such sins, as we have already told you and warned you. For God did not call us to be impure, but to live a holy life. Therefore, he who rejects this instruction does not reject man but God, who gives you His Holy Spirit,"* 1 Thessalonians 4:3-8.

To go from lust to love we need to know that the process of Biblical change is both putting off the old nature and putting on the new nature as described in Ephesians 4:22-24. Change happens specifically when old habits are replaced and not until then! Both the put-off and the put-on need to be accomplished in that order. Doing the put-on of love before getting rid of the put-off of lust is like putting perfume on a garbage pile. We need to get rid of the garbage of lust before we add the perfume of love.

### God directs us to changes that need to be made.

*"Let the husband render to his wife the affection due her, and likewise also the wife to her husband. The wife does not have authority over her own body, but the husband does. And likewise the husband does not have authority over his own body, but the wife does. Do not deprive one another except with consent for a time, that you may give yourselves to fasting and prayer; and come again together so that Satan may not tempt you*

*because of your lack of self-control" "I say to the unmarried ...if they cannot exercise self-control, let them marry. For it is better to marry than to burn with passion,"* 1 Corinthians 7:3-5 and 8-9, NKJV.

With these verses in mind we will look at three points:

**1. Self-sex or masturbation is not Christ-like behavior!**

This subject is a difficult one, but we need to talk about it because it is such a big problem. Is this practice sinful or not? I find it easier to ask another question to those who think this practice harmless. Would it be profitable to polish a brass knob on a sinking ship? No, the ship is going down and there are far more profitable things to do, like get in a lifeboat. Dear friend, Christ is the lifeboat that is far more profitable than pleasing self.

Various lust practices including pornography that people are hooked on, usually end up with this instant gratification practice. Once the habit is formed it quickly becomes a passion. *"Let the husband render to his wife the affection due her, and likewise also the wife to her husband,"* 1 Corinthians 7:3 NKJV. A married man or woman who seeks pleasure on their own will have less enthusiasm to embrace his or her spouse. What if God in Trinity didn't want to embrace us? Would we not be devastated and lonely? Looking at another woman or man with desire and then pleasing yourself sexually is wrong. Christ said, *"But I say to you that whoever looks at a woman to lust for her has already committed adultery with her in his heart,"* Matthew 5:28 NKJV. God also said, *"Do not lust after her beauty in your heart,"* Proverbs 6:25a NKJV. Another problem is, a young man who does these things will get so used to pleasing himself quickly that he will find it hard to be patient and wait for a wife to experience pleasure.

*"The wife does not have authority over her own body, but the husband does. And likewise the husband does not have authority over his own body, but the wife does,"* 1 Corinthians 7:4 NKJV. This verse shows that self-sex or masturbation is wrong. Jesus also said, *"If anyone would come after Me, he must deny himself and take up his cross and*

follow Me," Luke 9:23b NKJV. Paul said, *"Flee the evil desires of youth, and pursue righteousness, faith, love and peace, among with those who call on the Lord out of a pure heart,"* 2 Timothy 2:22. When we become more disciplined in one area of our lives, other area's will also fall into line!

Parents, talk to your children before someone else suggest they experience these things. Sexual addictions almost always begin in the teen years or even before and get worse quickly. Not talking about this according to the Word of God is foolish. Tell them the truth. Then pray and trust that the armor of God can win the battle!

## 2. Celibacy in marriage is not holy.

Contrary to some opinions, there is nothing "holy" about being celibate (not having sex) in marriage. *"Do not deprive each other except by mutual consent and for a time so that you may devote yourselves to prayer. Then come together again so that Satan will not tempt you because of your lack of self-control,"* 1 Corinthians 7:5. If a husband or wife both agree to stay apart for a time to pray – good. But, Paul warns, not for long so that lustful temptations are kept away.

## 3. Quantity verses quality

A major issue in 1 Corinthians 7:3-5 that most husbands are quick to point out is the frequency in intimacy, or quantity of sex. In the same verses, the wife is more likely to point to quality in the sexual relationship. Both are correct, and both desires must be met.

The words *"Let the husband render to his wife the affection due her,"* 1 Corinthians 7:3a NKJV, was particularly a message to men in a male-dominated culture. Remember, a wife needs affection. A hard-charging selfish man sees his wife as being there to please him. He will not see that he is also responsible to meet his wife's needs. A real husbandman takes the time to nurture and enjoy the vineyard.

### The wisdom of Job

*"There lived a man whose name was Job. This man was blameless and upright; he feared God and shunned evil,"* Job 1:1b. Job showed us how to move from lust to love. *"I made a covenant with my eyes not*

to look lustfully at a girl," Job 31:1. May God help us all to see that "lust" is a choice! Job made his choice and was called righteous!

## Young ladies

Girls, your purity is precious. It is a holy contract by covenant to God and your parents. Your purity is literally a picture of Christ and the Church (you). Don't break it! Young ladies, you have what a man wants, a cute body. Men will try to deceive you. They will pretend to be interested in a relationship with you for the purpose of stealing from you only what he really wants, physical intimacy. Things like hand-holding, a little hugging, and perhaps even a kiss may seem harmless to you. But it is only teasing him to go further. Next time he will want more than that. Remember lust is like that! Think this through! Do you really want a husband some day who is interested in getting physical with you, without seeing that you have spiritual, mental and emotional needs also? Encourage him in these areas!

Young ladies are giving their bodies to a man to try catch him for marriage. That's foolish! Think! If a man could get milk free, would he buy a cow? Many men are postponing marriage because they can get the goods without buying the ring. *"Like a gold ring in a pig's snout is a beautiful woman who shows no discretion,"* Proverbs 11:22.

Premarital sex is much like a bee draining a flower before it flies away to another flower in search of sweeter nectar. Guard yourself! Tell the man to buzz off. The flower is in bud, not bloom. Your virginity is part of the floral arrangement the bride privately gives to a bridegroom, after the ceremony. It is a woman with a gentle, quiet spirit and acts like a Christian who is irresistible to a Christian man! Giving in to premarital sex to get a husband, will likely give way to extramarital sex that will steal him away at a later time.

## Young men

Physical intimacy before marriage is lust not love. If you really love a young lady, you will want what is best for her! If you really love God, listen to His "NO." If you really love yourself, you will sinfully press for physical intimacy. Jesus said *"deny yourself,"* not please yourself. It was once foolishly said by a young man on a TV talk show, "I need to have sex and be a man." A wiser young man replied, "My dog has sex and it didn't make him no man." Amen!

A lustful person thinks sex before marriage, will put the fire out that is in you. No way! You will fan a flame that will quickly be a forest fire that even marriage will not put out. Love waits, because love sacrificially gives what is needed and is not self-serving. Premarital or extramarital sex is rebellion and bitterness against God and it is fornication. It is also idolatry because then you place self above God, saying His rules are not for you. Such a man mocks God and forfeits many blessings! The ones responsible for this girl are her Father in Heaven and her father or husband on earth. You do not have permission to trespass. Until a wedding ceremony, she is not yours.

### Both young men and women

If you get involved sexually before marriage, (even if you don't go all the way) then the physical part is what is mainly holding your relationship together. If the physical part is the main attraction, what do you think is going to happen if you progress to marriage? How will you deal with the other more complex relationship issues that are not sexually related? When two Christians are committed to God's rules, it is possible to become one – the goal of marriage. *"Seek first His kingdom and His righteousness,"* Matthew 6:33a, and you will be one with God and your spouse!

### A few points for young people seeking marriage.

1. **"Flee"**: God said, *"flee youthful lusts,"* not play around with lust.
2. **"Wait"**: *"I waited patiently for the Lord; He turned to me and heard my cry,"* Psalm 40:1. Wait for the Lord to give the right spouse.
3. **"Pray"**: *"Watch and pray, so that you will not fall into temptation,"* Matthew 26:41a.
4. **"Obey"**: *"Work out your salvation with fear and trembling, for it is God who works in you to will and to act according to His good purpose,"* Philippians 12b-13.

61

**5. "Be blessed":** *"Blessed is the man who does not walk in the counsel of the wicked,"* Psalm 1:1a.

**6. "Protection":** *"For the Lord God is a sun and a shield; the Lord bestows favor and honor; no good thing does He withhold from those whose walk is blameless,"* Psalm 84:11.

### Instruction to wives and husbands

A verse to husbands says, *"May you rejoice in the wife of your youth...may her breasts satisfy you always, may you ever be captivated by her love,"* Proverbs 5:18b-19. If a husband is not allowed to touch and be captivated by his wife's breasts and body, don't be too surprised when he looks at another woman. He is wrong when he does; but a wife is wrong for tempting him to do so! Husbands are commanded to *"rejoice in the wife!"* To *"rejoice"* is to have joy again and again. *"Godliness with contentment is great gain,"* 1 Timothy 6:6. A man or woman also lusts because they are not content or not thankful for what they have! Jealousy develops where true love is lacking!

### *"Always, may you ever be captivated by her love."*

*"Always"* is the wife to give the love, and *"always"* is the husband to be captivated by it. The word *"always"* includes a public show of affection by being courteous and respectful. Someone wisely said, "Sex begins in the kitchen," - meaning how a wife is treated outside the bedroom has implications for in the bedroom. *"Always,"* includes a private show of affection. *"Always"* is not for a week, month, or year, but until death. Our love for each other must increase through old age. As we loved each other's beauty and strength, so must we love each other's wrinkles and illnesses! For the Christian, marriage to Christ and to our spouse must *"always"* be getting better!

### Husbands and fathers need to wake up!

It is a husband's and father's responsibility to give affection and a solid emotional relationship to the wife and family. Women and little girls are concerned about relationships! If they do not have a good relationship in the home, they will be tempted to fall in different ways. The husband or father is responsible to give that affection. If a father or husband is so interested in their daily job that they ignore the wife or daughter, they may look elsewhere for a relationship. A daughter or wife getting into a wrong relationship is guilty of a grievous sin, but the father or husband is also responsible. He was commanded: *"Fathers, do not exasperate your children,"* Ephesians 6:4.

Talk to a young girl or woman involved in premarital or extramarital sex. You will find they want a real relationship, not sex. One of the greatest sins we fathers and husbands make in our home is neglecting relationships! We were appointed by God to be the bridegroom and father to show affection. Working hard is important, but it does not show the affection a wife or daughter needs. If we do not give it, the Kingdom of God is hurt significantly. We need to understand this to protect our "women" and have strong families.

It takes discipline or hard work to overcome all sinful habits. Study the following verses, confessing your sins as you go. Then, since lust must be replaced with love, do not repeat the sin, write out the specific steps that you will take to show love.

Leviticus 18:22-30 _____

Leviticus 20:12,13 _____

Psalm 119:9-11 _____

Proverbs 5:20-25 _____

Proverbs 18:10 _____

Proverbs 22:3, 24, 25 _____

Matthew 5:27-32 _____

Romans 1:24-32 _____

Romans 12:1-2 _____

Romans 13:11-14 _____

1 Corinthians 6:9-11 _____

2 Timothy 2:22 _____

# Chapter 8

# Reconciliation with God and Spouse

In this chapter, we will use examples of reconciliation issues other than just the marriage relationship. The process for repairing all relationships is really the same. Also, if we have problems with a teacher/student, employer/employee, or pastor/congregation relationship, it will affect our marriage. God's wisdom for reconciliation needs to be followed to get lasting results. God has given each of us a lifetime to repair our relationship with Him, and with others! He will judge us on it in The Judgment.

### A common problem

Two people were married for 20 years. The first 10 years were lovely. The last 10 were horrible. Add in the names, adjust the years, troubled marriages are like this! Jesus' 3-part counsel to the Ephesian church addressed this "cold" marriage problem. *"I hold this against you: You have forsaken your first love. (a) Remember the height from which you have fallen! (b) repent and (c) do the things you did at first. If you do not repent, I will come to you and remove your lampstand from its place,"* Revelation 2:4-5.

### *"Remember"*

First, *"remember."* Go back to the point that you were at when you began to fall. *"Remember"* what you did when things were going well. *"Remember"* how you spent time together. *"Remember"* how you looked at your spouse. *"Remember"* how you touched your spouse. *"Remember"* how you did things for them. Don't even peek at your spouse or point a finger at each other. *"First take the plank out of your own eye,"* Matthew 7:5a. God holds us responsible to change our own life. *"Remember the height from which you have fallen!"* In almost every failing marriage, the spouses only sees how the other has failed. Looking at your own life, changes marriages! Plus, God will only look at your life in The Judgment! This is an assignment from God. Write down all those things that you did when things were going well.

### *"Repent"*

Second, *"repent."* Confession is the first act of repentance. Confess your own sins or failures to love the Lord and your spouse. Don't think of telling others about your spouse's sin.  Confess your own. If you get up off your knees in prayer and are still thinking about what your spouse did to you, then the greatest need is to pray more until your attitude is corrected!

### *"Do"*

Third, *"do the things you did at first."* Do not just read this assignment! Do it; and your marriage will be blessed. We have a homework assignment for troubled marriages that works! It is God's Word and His will. It is hard to deny ourselves and die to self, but when we do, we are reminded, *"whoever loses his life for Me will save it,"* Luke 9:24. Living for self is what we naturally want to do and it ends in misery. Living for God and others is the narrow and difficult road, but it leads to life and happiness. We need to humble ourselves and walk that narrow road. Humble people are easy companions. Humility keeps a husband from being a tyrant. Humility promotes respect in the wife.

### Blaming others never solves any problem!

Reconciliation can only begin when our blame shifting ends. When we blame others for our personal problems, we show our ignorance! Others may tempt us but the problem is in our own heart! When we expect others to change but have no intention to change ourselves, we stand judged by God (1 Corinthians 11:31). When we each stand before God some day, the only issue will be, did we change? Pointing the finger at others in that day will not work, so why do it today? We have absolutely no excuse for not pursuing reconciliation with our spouse. If in Romans 12, we are commanded to love even our enemies, how much more does God expect us to love our spouses?

**Jesus told the truth.**

In a summary of the entire Bible, Jesus said we must *"love our neighbor."* Our spouse is our closest neighbor! If we are unwilling to love our spouse, we are unwilling to love God! *"If someone says, 'I love God' and hates his brother, he is a liar; for he who does not love his brother whom he has seen, how can he love God whom he has not seen,"* 1 John 4:20-21 NKJV? Jesus was even clearer when He said, *"If you forgive men when they sin against you, your Heavenly Father will also forgive you. But if you do not forgive men their sins, your Heavenly Father will not forgive your sins,"* Matthew 6:14-15.

Reconciliation is essentially made up of three parts: Confession + repentance + forgiveness = reconciliation. Keep these parts in mind because understanding them and putting them into practice is necessary to live the Christian life. We will first cover the confession part of reconciliation. In the next chapter we will look at the forgiveness and repentance part. We put these chapters in this book because there is no short cut to fixing relationship problems. We need to follow God's plans to fix them.

**Confession is the first part of reconciliation.**

The whole purpose of any confession is the need to be forgiven by God and man. Confession is foundational for a Christian. The neglect of this simple doctrine is such a big part of all marriage problems! Satan works overtime to lure us all away from Biblical confessions! Let us start with a Biblical definition. "Confession is agreeing with God about sins that you have committed against Him and against others, with a commitment to forsake those sins." Memorizing this definition is profitable. As we look at some points of a Biblical confession, we will see the abuses of it.

1. *"If we say that we have no sin, we deceive ourselves and the truth is not in us,"* **1 John 1:8 NKJV.**

Imagine a man or woman who lived a full life thinking their life was not sinful, only to stand before a righteous God in The Judgment to find out otherwise! What a waste of a life! The Word of God tells

67

us the truth about sin. If we fail to see our sinful thoughts, words and actions the same way God does, we will never progress to the next step of confessing it. Real wisdom comes when we understand how we have been living man's way instead of God's way. This means, we first need to see our adultery, anger, bitterness, drunkenness, fear, lust, and other problems as sinful! If we don't, we will never move to the next step of confessing it.

2. *"If we confess our sins, He is faithful and just and will forgive us our sins and purify us from all unrighteousness,"* 1 John 1:9 NKJV.

Think of how rebellious it is to see our sin as God does, and then not confess it. It is the nature of God to forgive all sin. But the IF means we have to do the confessing. No matter how much we have messed up in life, God wants to forgive us. May we humbly confess our sins.

3. **Saying "sorry" is not usually a confession.**

Sorry is usually the world's definition of confession, not God's. Saying to my friend, "I'm sorry, I was really mad at you yesterday," is not a confession! Three things are lacking! I did not clearly identify what I did wrong! I did not ask for forgiveness! I did not promise to repent! All three are the main purposes of confession and essential to reconciliation. The truth is, "sorry" usually focuses on our feelings. We must do more than feel differently! We must think, speak and act differently! God did much more than have a feeling for us! He sent a Savior. Jesus also came with a great action for us. He humbled Himself. He suffered. He died. These were all a sacrificial action for us. It is time we had a sacrificial action for others!

There is a correct way to use "sorry" in a confession. "My dear friend, I was wrong yesterday when I gossiped to the neighbor about how you fought with your husband. I am sorry that I hurt you. I was so wrong. I never want to do this again, but instead will say things that bless you in front of others. Will you forgive me for what I have done?" As you can see, this use of the word "sorry" did not omit our confession of the wrong. We asked for forgiveness and we promised to repent. Now we just need to follow through with a loving plan to be a blessing to our neighbor and fully repair the relationship.

**4. "Please forgive my sin," is not a confession either.**

By day's end, I had sinned against my wife five times. First, I was two hours late for her mother's birthday party. Second, my wife asked kindly where I was, and I shouted at her, "It is none of your business." Third, my wife cleaned the house well, and I did not say anything about it but complained about one window that was a bit dirty. Fourth, I watched a cricket match on TV for two hours, and I did not help her with the children. Fifth, I was angry with my wife because the children need to study more. In addition to these things, I did not pray with my wife or for my wife all day long.

With these sins in mind, I say to my wife at the end of the day, "Please forgive my sin." How unusual it would be if I only said that much in confession! But still, it is no confession at all! My wife's response should be, "Which sin are you confessing?" Simply saying "Please forgive my sin," confesses nothing. Worse yet, we go to God in prayer and pray, "Please forgive my sin," and confess nothing in particular! Because we confess nothing, we repent of nothing, and we repeat our sin again and again.

When we get SPECIFIC about what we do wrong, then we are serious about changing! We never change in generalities, but only when we get specific, thus serious. When we get specific, we finally agree with God about our sin and commit to change.

**5. My confession must not bring up another person's sin.**

When we confess our sin to another person, we are tempted to bring up what they did to us. We say to our son, "Why is the little neighbor boy crying?" Our son says, "He called me names, so I hit him with a stick." We then instruct our child that even if someone calls you names, it does not give you the right to hit them. We then tell our child, "Now, go and confess your sin to this little boy and ask for his forgiveness." The child obediently goes, and this is his or her confession, "Please forgive me for hitting you with a stick when you called me a 'dumb idiot'." Now his confession started fine, but as soon as the neighbor boy's wrong was brought up, our son was saying, "I had a good reason to do what I did." That is not a confession, as it puts the blame on the neighbor boy.

Even as adults, how often we comment throughout the day about what others did wrong to us and how little we talk about what we did wrong! The Biblical motive for confessing must be that we are 100% guilty, and that we cannot possibly ever make up for our wrong. So, we are seeking forgiveness to erase the guilt of our thoughts, words or actions from the ones we have hurt.

### 6. Don't let anyone stop your confession.

You were upset this morning and treated your best friend rudely. But, when you went to your friend to confess, she told you everything was fine, and that she was not really hurt by it. What must you do? Actually, this is an opportunity to witness to your friend. First, you must tell your friend all sin is serious and hurts God and other people! Your friends attempts to make you feel good instead of confessing, are really against God and you. If God says confess, and others say it is not necessary; God is the one who is right! We need God's and their forgiveness, not their sympathy. A Biblical confession shows the holiness of God and His hatred for sin.

### 7. What about saying, "I'll make it up to you"?

Can we do something "good" to make up for our sin? No. That is the opposite of a Biblical confession. For example, a man committed adultery. Aware that his wife found out, he picks up some flowers for her on his way home from his mistress. This husband will surely be wearing those flowers on his face! Why? He never said anything about his wrong! Instead he tried to make up for his sin by doing something good. God is even more disgusted at our good works to earn His favor. We need to understand that guilt needs forgiveness, and forgiveness needs a confession. The man in our example could never make up for his wrong even if he was perfect for the next 100 years. That is why we all need to confess and ask for our sin to be forgiven by God and man. What grace is ours if we humble ourselves and look to God and others for mercy instead of vainly thinking we can make up for our sin!

The words, "I will make it up to you" sound nice, but it shows a very wrong understanding of confession and forgiveness. If we think we can make up for sin by being extra "good," we do not even understand the Gospel! If we really can make up for what we did wrong by being extra nice, then why do we need to confess sin? The words, "I'll make up for my wrong," are self-righteous, manipulative, and even arrogant. We confess because we are guilty and cannot make up for the sin we have committed against God and others.

God in love shows us His total disgust with people trying to "work" their way back to Him or others saying, "*We are all like an unclean thing, and all our righteousnesses are like filthy rags,*" Isaiah 64:6 NKJV. The filthy rags in this verse are a woman's bloody cloth. By thinking, "my blood, my sweat, my tears, my efforts will make up for my sin and make me right with God," we reject God's gift of His Son's blood. God is not satisfied with our blood, but His Son's perfect blood!

Adam could not even make up for even one sin by his works in plucking a leaf in Genesis 3:7. Yet we somehow think we can work hard and God will love us and in the end forgive us. We not only need the grace and forgiveness of God, we also need the forgiveness of others. That is exactly why we confess and ask for mercy! Then, in gratitude, we must do many good works, after the confession!!

## 8. There is only one Mediator to carry our confession to God.

Many believe we can go through some holy saint who is either dead or living to get to Jesus or God. Some even think we can go through Jesus' mother. The Bible does not support this. We can only receive forgiveness from God by going through one Mediator alone: Jesus Christ. Jesus said, "*I tell you the truth, I am the gate for the sheep,*" John 10:7. "*I am the door. If anyone enters by Me, he will be saved, and will go in and out and find pasture,*" John 10:9 NKJV. Many people are trying to get to God through other doors.

71

"There is one God and one Mediator between God and men, the man Christ Jesus," 1 Timothy 2:5. A sinner cannot possibly mediate for another sinner. Jesus said, "I am the way and the truth and the life. No one comes to the Father except through Me," John 14:6. Jesus is the only provision God gave us to have our sins forgiven. "The Son of man has authority on earth to forgive sins," Mark 2:10b. The church cannot forgive sin. Jesus forgives. The church cannot save. Jesus saves. As great as the Apostle Peter was, he was still the "little rock" and can not forgive sin. Jesus is "the Rock" or cornerstone. The song is true, "On Christ, the solid Rock, I stand, all other ground is sinking sand." Peter himself testified about Jesus, "To Him all the prophets witness that, through His name, whoever believes in Him will receive remission of sins," Acts 10:43 NKJV. That's why we end a prayer, "in Jesus' name I pray."

Some say clergy and priests have the power to forgive or not to forgive sin based on John 20:23. "If you forgive the sins of any, they are forgiven them; if you retain the sins of any they are retained," John 20:23 NKJV. This verse can never be interpreted without using the rest of the Bible. In John 20:23, the disciples were given the responsibility to supervise or guard the true church. In Matthew 18, we learn this responsibility in more detail. There are four steps of supervision guidelines in Matthew 18:15-17. A summary and words of encouragement are in Matthew 18:18-20. Notice how this summary is literally the same as John 20:23.

> "Assuredly, I say to you, whatever you bind on earth will be bound in Heaven, and whatever you loose on earth will be loosed in Heaven. Again, I say to you that if two of you agree on earth concerning anything that they ask, it will be done for them by My Father in Heaven. For where two or three are gathered together in My name. I am there in the midst of them," Matthew 18:18-20.

**9. Confession is not telling God something He doesn't know.**

In confessing, we never tell God something He doesn't already know. He sees everything! A real confession takes personal responsibility for sinning and openly admits to God and others that we are sick of going man's way in life, and want to go God's way.

In all these points we are not teaching that it is the quality of our confession that saves us. It is the quality of the sacrifice of Christ on the Cross that forgives! Even the weakest plea to Him for forgiveness will be heard. Biblical confessions are serious about repentance, call for forgiveness, and always look for reconciliation. A Biblical confession is an act of worship that clearly sees the holiness of God and His hatred for sin. God's kingdom and our marriages will advance, and we will also be blessed, as we implement Biblical confessions.

# Chapter 9

# Repentance and Forgiveness

Many people wonder why they can't change. It is because we are born slaves to sin and need to be changed. Others will say, "I go to church regularly and I still don't change." We are slaves to sin and need to be changed. Biblical repentance is a new change of direction in thoughts, words or actions by which our minds/hearts have been changed from living by the deeds of the flesh and pleasing self, to living by the Spirit and pleasing God and others. The world can also change without God. But they merely change one unbiblical habit for another unbiblical habit. Biblical change or repentance is a result of a sovereign work of grace whereby our new hearts have a stronger desire to follow God's way of obedience rather than man's way of disobedience. If the Gospel has not changed us, then the grace of God is not yet in us. New loving habits are God's grace flowing out of us!

It is so sad, Satan is having such a great time watching the various denominations and individuals fight about somewhat minor issues, while failing to preach or live the gospel of grace and repentance – major issues! Jesus said that the time has come, *"The kingdom of God is near. Repent and believe the good news,"* Mark 1:15. Again in the last book of the Bible Jesus said, *"Be earnest, and repent,"* Revelation 3:19b.

### Actions speak louder than words.

John the Baptist called the religious community of his day, a *"brood of vipers."* They were biting and devouring one another instead of reconciling. Then in a stern warning, he said, *"Bear fruits worthy of repentance, and do not begin to say to yourselves, we have Abraham as our father,"* Luke 3:8 NKJV. This verse is also a big warning to us! So many people claim to know much about the grace of God, but fail to be gracious in how they treat others. Such people know almost nothing about grace!

75

**Biblical change is a process clearly presented in Ephesians 4.**

*"You were taught with regard to your former way of life, to put off your old self which is being corrupted by its deceitful desires, to be made new in the attitude of your minds and put on the new self, created to be like God in true righteousness and holiness,"* Ephesians 4:22-24. The putting-off the old and putting-on the new is what repentance is all about.

**God gives us examples of how to change.**

*"Each of you must put off falsehood and speak truthfully to his neighbor,"* Ephesians 4:25a. The "put-off" of lying, must be done first. Then it must be replaced by speaking truthfully. The heart is not changed until the new Biblical put-on is accomplished.

God gives us another example: *"He who has been stealing* (put-off) *must steal no longer* (put-off), *but must work* (first put-on), *doing something useful with his own hands, that he may have something to share* (second put-on) *with those in need,"* Ephesians 4:28.

God gives us yet one more example to teach us the process of repentance. *"Do not let any unwholesome talk come out of your mouths,* (put-off) *but only what is helpful for building others up* (put-on) *according to their needs,"* Ephesians 4:29a.

A key to sustained change is to focus on the put-on! This point needs to be emphasized. But don't forget to dump the garbage first. In the reconciliation process, a repentant life removes reminders of sins. The reason is, sins that are unresolved in the past, remain strong temptations to sin again in the present.

**The benefits of repentance**

Working diligently on personal repentance has three benefits for reconciliation. First, our minds are renewed by the Spirit of God when our thoughts, words and actions are Biblical and good (Colossians 3:10). Second, when others see a new spirit in us, they will know we are ready and willing to reconcile with God and anyone else. Third, taking the log or sin out of our own lives helps us see clearly to do evangelism and discipleship.

Don't wait until you feel like it to work on repentance. Do it regardless of how you feel. Going against our natural feelings is what the Christian life is all about if we will *"bear fruits worthy of repentance,"* Luke 3:8 NKJV. We are no better than the Pharisees if we fail to repent. Instant gratification is the goal of worldly living, not Christian living! Disciplined obedience is the hallmark of a Christian.

### Forgiveness is the third part of reconciliation.

Why do we claim to love God but cannot stand certain Christians? Still others claim to be a Christian, but hate their spouse.

*"If anyone says, 'I love God,' yet hates his brother, he is a liar. For anyone who does not love his brother, whom he has seen, cannot love God, whom he has not seen. And He has given us this command: Whoever loves God must also love his brother,"* 1 John 4:20-21.

But, how must I love my spouse or others? God tells us by forgiving them and He even tells us why it is so important!

*"For if you forgive men their trespasses, your heavenly Father will also forgive you. But if you do not forgive men their trespass, neither will your heavenly Father forgive your trespasses,"* Matthew 6:14-15 NKJV.

Forgive others, or forego God's fatherly forgiveness of you. But, how do we forgive others? God tells us, we must be, *"forgiving each other just as in Christ God forgave you,"* Ephesians 4:32. This brings the two biggest points on forgiveness. First, we need to understand the forgiveness of God. Second, we need to copy the forgiveness of God. This kind of study follows the book of Ephesians. The first three chapters tell how we were saved by grace and the final three chapters, what our response must be.

### Understanding the forgiveness of God.

We were told to forgive others *"just as in Christ God forgave you,"* Ephesians 4:32. We will now look very closely at exactly how

God forgave us when He saved us. How we were forgiven by God in the salvation process is too often a big argument in many churches. Some Christians say, "I chose God when I made a decision for him." Others say, "God chose me." Actually, both are right. Don't argue with the person who says, "I chose God," simply ask them, "Why did you chose God?" There is only one answer: The Holy Spirit convicted them of their sin and put them down on their knees. The Holy Spirit is God choosing them. A person does choose God, after God chooses them. To understand forgiveness we need to understand this and then forgive others in the same way. We will look at some passages that show how God, in grace, chose us.

Ephesians 1:4 - *"He chose us in Him before the creation of the world."*
Ephesians 1:5 - *"He predestined us to be 'adopted.'* In the adoption process, who chooses whom?
Ephesians 1:9- *"He made known to us the mystery of His will according to His good pleasure."*
Ephesians 1:11 *"In Him we were also chosen."*

From Ephesians one, we see that in grace, God the Father planned our salvation. In grace, the Holy Spirit convicted us of our sin. In grace Christ redeemed us. In grace, the Trinity as one God worked together to accomplish our forgiveness, all moving towards us.

In Ephesians two, we see that in verses one and five we were *"dead."* A dead man does not move to Christ! In such a rotten, stinking, sinful condition, I could not prove to God, that I deserved to be forgiven because I was *"dead."* Likewise, others do not need to repent first before we forgive them!

God forgave me when I was His *"enemy"* in Romans 5:10. Since God forgave me when I was His enemy, I must forgive my enemy. I must forgive others *"just as in Christ God forgave you."* Since God forgave me when I was a dead, rotten sinner, I must forgive other rotten sinners! Since God gave me what I needed: grace and love, instead of what I deserved: death, I must give others what they need not what they deserve! Since God covers my sin Psalm 32:1, and puts

78

it behind His back (Isaiah 38:17b,) I must do the same. Since God doesn't forget about my sin but chooses to *"remember it against me no more,"* Ezekiel 18:22 & Psalm 32:2. I must do the same.

For those who think God forgets our sin, look at the last verse in the book of Ecclesiastes. *"For God will bring every deed into judgment, including every hidden thing, whether it is good or evil."* God will not forget our sin, since in The Judgment it will all come up again, but it will not be against us! It will be against Christ, if we are a Christian. At first we may not be able to forget someone's wrong either, nor do we need to. In the next paragraph we will see what we must do.

### Copying the forgiveness of God

Forgiveness from God to us is three things and thus forgiveness from us to others must also be three things.

First, as a Christian, God never brings my sin against me in person again as it is now on Christ. I must not bring up the sins of others against them either, even though I remember what they did.

Second, God never tells others about my sin, thus I must not gossip and tell others about what someone has done to me either.

Third, God never dwells on my sin once He has forgiven me, for then He would be holding it against me. Likewise, when I am supposed to be sleeping at night, I must not dwell on my neighbor's sin either, as then I am holding it against them in my mind.

If I forgive as God does, I will soon forget what someone has done to me. Forgiving like God does promotes reconciliation. Even if we did no wrong to a fellow brother, we are still responsible to forgive him and be reconciled to him. In fact, it is so important that Jesus said, *"Leave your gift there before the altar, and go your way. First be reconciled to your brother, and then come and offer your gift,"* Matthew 5:24 NKJV. Meditate on these important points!

### The sacrificial love of God in repairing a relationship is vastly different from man's way.

Man's wisdom says, "Leave a person alone if they don't love you and just ignore them." Jesus left the 99 sheep in the sheep-pen and forgave and reconciled and loved me, when I was a lost and wandering sheep (Matthew 18:12). A believer's refusal to forgive was met with an angry master (Jesus) who handed a Christian over to the torturers (Satan's little followers) until the believer was ready to forgive (Matthew 18:34). Jesus taught that forgiving another was a matter of simple obedience and not exemplary faith (Luke 17:3-10). Even though we do not feel like forgiving, we must, or Jesus will not forgive us (Matthew 6:14,15).

For those who have been greatly sinned against by your spouse or another person, meditate on how God in Christ forgives! All Christians were greatly sinning before salvation, and deserved death, (Romans 6:23). But God gave us what we needed: life, not what we deserved: death. Brother and sister, to forgive someone is to give them what they need! Do they deserve it? NO! Neither did you or I deserve God's forgiveness.

We must forgive all sin no matter how devastating it has been! As you gasp in shock, remember Ephesians 4:32. We absolutely must forgive as God has forgiven us. Does not God forgive all of our sins? He is merely asking us to do something that He has already done for us. Yes, we must forgive even our enemies since we were God's enemies when He forgave us. Now God is asking us to give our neighbor what God gave us. Married people, your closest neighbor is your spouse! Peace and reconciliation is possible with God and with others when we are busy *"forgiving each other just as in Christ God forgave you,"* Ephesians 4:32.

### Sin has consequences.

Do not think that just because all sin must be forgiven that sin does not have any consequences. There are physical and material consequences of sin. If a man steals money from a bank and then confesses his sin, God and maybe even the bank will forgive him. But, the police may haul him off to jail (physical), and he may need to pay a fine (material). A man may get drunk and break a leg in an accident (physical). God will forgive his sin if he confesses it, but the leg will still be broken and he may have some medical bills (material).

In the Bible, David sinned with Bathsheba. When David finally confessed his sin of adultery and murder, he was forgiven. But, as a consequence the baby still died. If my son has a big fight with the neighbor boy and he comes to me and says, "Sorry." I must forgive him. But, I must still lovingly discipline him (physical), or he will learn to give a false confession just to escape discipline, and I would then make a Pharisee.

## Conclusion

We can be so proud of the fact that we believe in the grace and forgiveness of God, and then neglect to be gracious in practice. Who truly believes in grace? Is it the one who has more knowledge of what grace is, in their head? Or is it the one who puts grace into practice in their life? The answer is clear, and this has everything to do with forgiveness leading to reconciliation. *"Search me, O God, and know my heart; test me and know my anxious thoughts. See if there is any offensive way in me, and lead me in the way everlasting,"* Psalm 139:23-24. May we fall on our knees, remembering the sober fact that our righteousness must exceed the righteousness of the Pharisees who were a *"brood of vipers."*

# Chapter 10

# Marriage Conflicts

## 1. Specific problems that wives have

### A. Wives need to show respect.

The most common Biblical counseling problem comes from a Christian wife who is without hope. She has an unbelieving, cruel husband and pleads, "What can I do?" God's advice is this:

> "*Wives, in the same way, be submissive to your husbands so that, if any of them do not believe the Word, they may be won over without words by the behavior of their wives,*" 1 Peter 3:1.

It is easy for a Christian wife to think, "I will not submit to or respect my husband because he is cruel and unbelieving." Even a Christian wife mistakenly thinks that it is her harsh husband, that is her biggest problem in life. NO! God knows, her biggest problem is still her own heart! God wants her to know that husbands are driven away from the Gospel when a wife demands that he must change the way he lives but she makes no real attempt to change her own life!

God summarized many verses on marriage in Ephesians 5 with this counsel for every wife. "*Let the wife see that she respects her husband,*" Ephesians 5:33b NKJV. Yes, "*respect*" is a primary area that wives are especially commanded to be obedient in. The dictionary defines respect as "an attitude of admiration or esteem." But the Bible shows that respect is more than an attitude; it is an act of love by the way a wife treats a husband.

### B. Gossip is not respect.

An idle wife who is busy with gossip is not wise! "*A gossip separates close friends,*" Proverbs 16:28b. A husband and wife are supposed to be the closest of friends here on earth! So when a wife has "loose lips," she separates herself from her husband. The slander of her husband is disrespectful. Why does she tell of her husband's mistakes to those who cannot help, or have no reason to know? Such words of complaint to others are really an act of self-pity or self-love on her part. This wife is really looking for others to applaud her for being such a martyr. She surely does not fully realize that the guilt of her sin of being such a gossip, keeps bitterness in her heart. Along with the anger in her speech, shame and sadness will be is her real reward. We underlined the wife's sins to make them clear.

With such an attitude, it should not come as a surprise when this wife is depressed! The husband may have hurt her, but her response of trying to get even with her husband only lets her husband continue to hurt her. Thinking negative thoughts about a husband will never bring peace of mind! The very peace that this wife is seeking with her husband will not be hers.

Christian counsel to a gossiping woman is quite different from the counsel of the world! The world would agree with her that she needs to love herself more and even separate from this man. The world tells her to elevate herself above her husband, and show him who is boss. Biblical counsel would tell a gossiping and bitter woman to first take the log out of her own eye; then she will be able to see clearly how to help her husband (Matthew 7:1-5) and that her bitterness is actually demonic (James 3:14-15).

### C. Gentleness shows respect.

"Brothers, if someone is caught in a sin, you who are spiritual should restore him gently," Galatians 6:1a. Quite simply, "gentleness" shows respect. God has so designed husbands to be respected, and the wife must be the number one source of that respect! A wife will never be able to respect and elevate her husband until she first lowers herself! A wife who moans and groans about her husband's lack of leadership is partially responsible for it. Encouraged to lead in even the smallest areas of life, the husband may lead in other areas of life also. Amazingly, when God and the husband are honored, a wife's bitterness and depression will soon be lifted!

### D. Harsh speech and actions drive a husband away.

God is well aware of how a harsh husband abuses his wife. God clearly sees the abandonment of the husband, the drunkenness, and the beatings. But, if the wife reacts to all this with bitterness, she is not any better! God's view of this troubled marriage is a *"demonic"* wife , James 3:15, pointing a finger at a sinning husband demanding that he change. A woman with bitter, harsh speech provokes a man to flee her along with certain responsibilities. *"Better to live on a corner of the roof than share a house with a quarrelsome wife,"* Proverbs 21:9. A man with a drinking problem, or even a husband who is working too much, may be more comfortable in the bar or at work. He does not want to go to his own home to face an angry wife. *"It is better to dwell in the wilderness, than with a contentious and angry woman,"* Proverbs 21:19 NKJV.

It should not come as a surprise then to see that a Christian wife is to be submissive even to an unbelieving husband. She is called by God to love him by submitting, thus showing the love of Christ. This particular theology however is not only for wives. It is also true for husbands, which we shall see later.

### E. Good conduct wins over a husband.

A Biblical wife can win over even an unbelieving, pagan husband without uttering a word because conduct, not speech, changes husbands! Underneath every husband's hard shell is a man waiting to be loved and appreciated! Acts of love really do speak louder than words.

> *"When they observe your chaste conduct accompanied by fear. Do not let your beauty be that outward adorning of arranging the hair, of wearing gold, or of putting on fine apparel; but let it be the hidden person of the heart, with the incorruptible ornament of a gentle and quiet spirit, which is very precious in the sight of God. For in this manner, in former times, the holy women who trusted in God also adorned themselves, being submissive to their own husbands,"* 1 Peter 3:2-6 NKJV.

By putting on ornaments of a gentle, quiet spirit, a woman is most pleasing to both God and man. A reasonably attractive woman on the outside with a gentle, quiet spirit on the inside, is irresistible to a man. Remember, real beauty in a woman begins with a beautiful heart and radiates to the face and many kind actions. That is exactly what this passage is teaching. God knows real beauty and wants to open our eyes to it. A beautiful woman on the outside with a harsh and bitter heart may work well as a model in a magazine, but she is not fit to live with.

### F. A wife is *"called"* to be like *"Christ."*

The words *"in the same way,"* 1 Peter 3:1a in the NIV, is translated *"likewise"* in the NKJV. These words connect the reader to some teaching that comes before this verse. When we turn to 1 Peter 2, we see that the wife must be like a *"slave,"* and like *"Christ."*

> *"Slaves, submit yourselves to your masters with all respect, not only to those who are good and considerate, but also to those who are harsh. For it is commendable if a man bears up under the pain of unjust suffering because he is conscious of God. But how is it to your credit if you receive a beating for doing wrong and endure it? But if you suffer for doing good and you endure it, this is commendable before God. To this you were called, because Christ suffered for you, leaving you an example, that you should follow in His steps,"* 1 Peter 2:18-21.

### Christ modeled submissiveness through obedience.

Being submissive is not being a doormat but humbly serving others. The word "serve" is part of the word servant. A servant is required to be obedient in what they do, whether they feel like it or not! A wife is never a hypocrite when she is submissive and does things that she does not feel like doing. A person is a hypocrite when they do something they do not enjoy doing and then say that they enjoyed it. A wife may not feel like cooking a meal, cleaning the house, cleaning up a child, or even having sex with her husband. But she does it anyway, as an act of love, for the purpose of serving. True love is all about being submissive and having a servant heart.

### Jesus never threatened.

*"When they hurled their insults at him, he did not retaliate; when he suffered, he made no threats. Instead, He entrusted Himself to Him who judges justly,"* 1 Peter 2: 23. Instead of threatening, Jesus trusted in God to change the hearts of others. When the husband yells and does not treat the wife in a proper way and the wife's response is quiet and respectful, she leaves room for the Holy Spirit to convict

the husband of his guilt. On the other hand, when a wife retaliates with anger and bitterness, a sinful husband quickly justifies his wrong actions by returning evil for evil.

**G. A wife's secret to real peace is in following Jesus' example.**

Jesus remained patient when He was mistreated! He waited for God to change the offender. That's the key. Don't impatiently wait for your husband to change, but patiently for Jesus to change your husband. There is a big difference! Jesus knew the truth expressed in Ezekiel 36:23-38, that only God can change a human heart. She must pray and wait patiently for that!

A woman with a cruel husband can be at peace! She must do her daily work for God first and then to please her husband second. Then she will know peace. When her work and life is worship to God, she can wait for God to change her husband. This is not to suggest a wife is not to ever lovingly rebuke her husband. She is to rebuke, but to do so gently, and only after she is willing to change her own faults. The point here is that a wife can be at peace — even if her husband is not! When the husband sees Christ in her, he hopefully will want her Christ.

### Wives in review

*"Wives, submit to your own husbands, as to the Lord. For the husband is the head of the wife, as also Christ is the head of the church; and He is the Savior of the body. Therefore, just as the church is subject to Christ, so let the wives be to their own husbands in everything,"* Ephesians 5:22-24 NKJV.

Problems come when the wife attempts to play the role that her husband has been given by God. A clear command is: "Wives, submit to your husbands." This verse does not say wives "should submit." It is an absolute truth, not subject to debate. We have seen, a wife must even submit to an unbiblical husband in 1 Peter 3:1. A wife must submit to her "own" husband, not any other man. "In everything," a wife is to submit not just in some things, but just as the Church is to submit to Christ in everything.

A wife who has failed to submit has been unwilling to live for her husband. Domineering wives fail to submit when they do not let their husband lead. Then she complains to others that her man is not a good leader in the home. If any Christian tried to replace Christ as the head of the Church, it would be idolatry. A wife is far from innocent when she will not submit to her husband. Unless her husband asks her to lie, cheat, or steal, etc., she must respectfully submit to his headship.

## 2. Specific problems that husbands have.

*"Likewise you husbands, dwell with them with understanding, giving honor to the wife, as to the weaker vessel, and as being heirs together of the grace of life, that your prayers may not be hindered,"* 1 Peter 3:7 NKJV.

The word *"likewise"* again points to instruction that comes before this verse. The husband is instructed here to be like the wife, like Jesus and like the servant in 1 Peter 2:18 - 3:6. The husband has one more verse than his wife does because he is the head of the house.

### A. *"Dwell with them with understanding,"* 1 Peter 3:7a.

One of the greatest complaints unhappy wives give is: "my husband doesn't listen to me." A husband who does not listen to his wife cannot possibly *"understand"* his wife. He is not even listening to his own body that needs attention! Even our own head listens to a leg that has pain by telling the arm to rub the leg. The husband's communication needs to improve!

### How does a husband improve his listening skills?

First, we husbands don't listen because we are self-centered! To listen, we need to deny ourselves before we can listen to our wife, or any other person. Active listening means we must tune out the T.V. and tune in the wife. If we would rather hold the remote control of the T.V. in the evening instead of the hand of our wife, we are not ready to listen. Only one has a soul! Isn't it strange, when we would rather go to the coffee shop and talk to those we don't know, than talk to our spouse! Listening to the wife is eternally important. God clearly said in 1 John 4, that if I do not love my neighbor whom I can see, then I cannot say that "I love God" whom I cannot see. Since a wife is a husband's closest neighbor, how can we love a wife if we will not listen to them?

Jesus delights to hear our prayers and problems. A husband is commanded to be like Christ. Do we delight to hear our wife's problems and petitions? Jesus said to the Church, "*Come to Me, all you who are weary and burdened, and I will give you rest,*" Matthew 11:28. When our wives are weary and burdened, are we willing to give them rest? May we learn from Jesus who said, "*Take my yoke upon you and learn from me, for I am gentle and humble in heart, and you will find rest for your souls,*" Matthew 11:29.

A husband is listening when he can summarize what his wife has just said. It is so easy to open my mouth to my wife and say, "I love you," and moments later have my ears closed to what she is saying! It is he who listens that is willing to "*esteem others as better than himself,*" Philippians 2:3b NKJV. How easy it is to ask my wife a question to which she gives a polite answer. Then two hours later I ask the same question again! Why? Because I did not listen! The two-edged sword of the Word cuts us deep sometimes, and it should! A person who is speaking to us always needs and appreciates respectful attention. You may be thinking, "My wife talks all the time, and if I summarize what she says, it will be a full time job." Well, maybe our wife talks too much because we listen too little. Husbands who communicate better during the day communicate better at night.

**B. "*Give honor to the wife, as to the weaker vessel,*" 1 Peter 3:7b.**

Some versions say "*precious vase*" instead of "*weaker vessel.*" A 2000 year-old, precious vase from China would be a "*weaker vessel,*" fragile, and also a "*precious vase.*" Since an expensive vase could be easily broken, we would never drop it or be rough with it. We surely would treat it with respect and honor, even place it on a shelf for all to see and admire. A bride is adorned for a husband to be honored and admired. When she becomes a wife, she still needs to be honored and admired! The problem we husbands have is that we cannot elevate and honor our wife until we first remove ourselves from the top shelf. "*Honor*" encourages respect!

A sinning husband is like a big hammer. How else do I not honor my "*precious vase*" wife? A husband's personality can be like a 10-kilo hammer. What happens when a big hammer gets into a disagreement with a "*precious vase*" wife? The hammer SMASHES the vase, wins the argument, and leaves home bragging to his friends how he put his wife in her place. Meanwhile, the precious vase is crying, severely broken, and is depressed. A precious vase that is broken is without honor, not very beautiful, and the husband is responsible for its condition. Wives come packaged with a warning, "Caution, easily broken if not handled with care." We are reminded that, *"The Lord is acting as the witness between you and the wife of your youth, because you have broken faith with her, though she is your partner, the wife of your marriage covenant,"* Malachi 2:14b.

### C. *"Heirs together of the grace of life,"* 1 Peter 3:7c.

God reminds the husband that a wife goes through life with the same difficulties and trials he is facing. Thus he must both sympathize with her and treat her with compassion. Humility promotes compassion. Any husband that refuses to be humble can never be compassionate. It is the world that tells a man to assert himself, not God! Never think that threatening is a good way to keep authority over a wife. If a gentle approach will not work, then the husband is lost in this world and in the next. A husband's *"pride only breeds quarrels, but wisdom is found in those who take advice,"* Proverbs 13:10. A biblical husband is willing to take advice from his wife and this is part of what it means to be humble. On the other hand, a proud husband could not even have compassion with an angel of a wife, but a humble husband can honor, love and respect any wife!

### D. *"That your prayers may not be hindered,"* 1 Peter 3:7d NKJV.

A husband who is not treating his wife correctly has his prayers hindered. Why? You may remember that in Psalm 66:18, David said, *"If I had cherished sin in my heart, the Lord would not have listened."* With this truth in mind, we can see why God in His wisdom required a man to be an obedient servant in the home before he was qualified to serve and lead in the church effectively as a pastor, elder, or deacon. *"Hindered"* prayers by those in church leadership, do not advance the kingdom of God in the church or in the home!

> *"If we claim to have fellowship with Him yet walk in the darkness, we lie and do not live by the truth. But if we walk in the light, as He is in the light, we have fellowship with one another, and the blood of Jesus, His Son, purifies us from all sin. If we claim to*

be without sin, we deceive ourselves and the truth is not in us. If we confess our sins, He is faithful and just and will forgive us our sins and purify us from all unrighteousness. If we claim we have not sinned, we make Him out to be a liar and His Word has no place in our lives," 1 John 1:6-10.

### Ways that the husband is not a proper head of the wife.

"The husband is the head of the wife, as also Christ is head of the church; and He is the Savior of the body," Ephesians 5:23 NKJV. This verse is equally instructive for husbands and wives. This verse does not say that the husband should be the head of the wife. The husband is the head of the wife. A husband can be a poor head of a wife in two ways, but he can never stop being the head.

First, many husbands are "bad" guys who physically abuse their wives, just the opposite of saving and protecting them. This condition is very common outside the church. When a man beats his wife, he beats his own body. How dumb! What head would bite and devour its own body? Answer - one that is proud and hungry for trouble.

Second, many husbands can appear to be "nice" guys, but yet they are running away from their headship responsibilities. This condition is very common in the church. It is harmful for God's kingdom and torture for the wife! Christ never ran away from His responsibility to save and serve His body, the Church! Christ humbly came, suffered, died, and secured the salvation of the Church. In such a way, the husband as the head of the wife must give himself for her. He is to protect her body and soul as the savior of the body. Christ's grace must guide a home just as much as God's commandments must govern it. I have seen so many heads of households run their homes without grace and think they are good, Biblical examples! Much law and little grace is a Pharisee at work.

*"**Husbands, love your wives,** just as Christ also loved the church and gave Himself for it, that He might sanctify and cleanse it with the washing of water by the word, that He might present it to Himself a glorious church, not having spot or wrinkle or any such thing but that it should be holy and without blemish,* Ephesians 5:25-27 NKJV.

Christ loved the Church by serving it, cleansing it, protecting it, all the time sanctifying it, grooming it to perfection. Some husbands find a wife that is lovely, and then provoke them to be ugly, and then blame the wife for her ugliness. Depression, fear, worry, anger, and bitterness are good examples of how a wife's beauty is not right. And yes, the husband is responsible, just as our head is responsible to protect the body from these things. Christ found an ugly sinner, and with a great action made the sinner beautiful and rejoices in his/her beauty! Christ lived for the Church. Many husbands live for themselves.

## 3. Biblical communication for all of us

### A. Our words show our level of spiritual growth or lack of it.

Our words clearly reflect our intent to heal or to hurt others! So often we may be absolutely right in what we say, but very wrong in how we say it. In such a case, we are still wrong! If ever we are going to change any relationship, we need to learn how to speak! Someone once very wisely said, "Speaking the truth without love is like doing surgery without anesthesia."

> *"I tell you that men will have to give account on the Day of Judgment for every careless word they have spoken. For by your words you will be acquitted, and by your words you will be condemned,"* Matthew 12: 36-37.

The book of James compares our tongue to a rudder on a ship. As the rudder turns, so goes the ship. Indeed, we cut God and man down with our words, and in the process hurt ourselves also. *"The tongue is so set among our members that it defiles the whole body,"* James 3:6 NKJV.

### B. Rebuke gently and privately!

From time to time, a very loving rebuke is needed. In these times we must keep in mind, *"Love covers over a multitude of sins,"* I Peter 4:8b. Just as a knife dulls with constant use, so does a constant rebuke. Rebuke must be sparingly used, and only in proportion to praises that are given. An old Puritan minister, the Rev. Richard Steele said:

> "True love requires rebuke, but it must be given with the greatest wisdom and tenderness imaginable, not before

strangers, rarely before the family, mainly for sins, seldom for anything else."

If the portion of rebuke is too strong, it will do more harm than good! Job, a righteous man, left us a good example of a rebuke when he simply said to his wife, *"You are talking like a foolish woman,"* Job 2:10. A rebuke should be short and sweet. A mild reproof is more likely to produce a sincere repentance. A strong rebuke is more likely to produce bitterness. It was said of Jesus, *"He will not quarrel nor cry out, nor will anyone hear His voice in the streets,"* Matthew 12:19NKJV. If our voice of rebuke is heard *"in the streets,"* we are not following Christ example!

### C. Encourage much and publicly!

One of the biggest problems when relationships go sour is that we have a tendency to see only the wrong in another person and not any of the good. How often I have wrongly done this. It is not a good way to disciple a child, a student, a congregation member, a worker or a wife. Such a way of managing relationships is quicker to make someone bitter instead of better! When we rebuke often and praise little, we have it backwards, and it is no wonder our relationships are on a downward slide. When people sense they are rejected in our presence, they will be quick to find an exit.

Key to real change is looking for the good, and commenting on these things. Paul said, *"Let your conversation be always full of grace, seasoned with salt, so that you may know how to answer everyone,"* Colossians 4:6. It is particularly important for all managers to be the number one cheerleader in the business, church, and school. However, it will be hard to do if they do not practice it in the home. If I were to list the counseling problems where the leader in the business, church, school or home was a bear, it would be a book in itself. Never forget, fears and threats are able to motivate but love and encouragement does it God's way!

When Hannah was really hurting emotionally and physically, it was the kind and gracious words of her husband Elkanah, that brought her to dinner in I Samuel 1:8-9. Our words will heal a relationship when our talk, *"is helpful for building others up according to their needs, that it may benefit those who listen,"* Ephesians 4:29b.

93

# Chapter 11

# Love and Respect Sums up Marriage

Ephesians 5 ends with a one-verse summary on marriage. *"Each one of you must also love his wife as he loves himself, and the wife must respect her husband,"* Ephesians 5:33. We husbands are especially to see to it that we *"love"* our wives. Wives are to see that she "respects her husband. *"Love"* and respect are the solution for new marriages and for troubled marriages also. We will look at two failing marriages and see how *"love"* and respect were the cure. If you for some reason think that there is no hope for your marriage then, you need a vision of your marriage as God shows us they can be.

### 1. God addresses husbands.

A husband can change his marriage! The one thing he can give to his wife is himself. Are you willing to do that? A man who had a troubled marriage said he would die for his wife. The counselor told him, "You need to start living for your wife, not die for her." This husband must do more than work his fingers to the bone for his wife! A husband can win the respect of his wife by his wisdom and affection he shows to her. The failure of every man to live for his wife is essentially a failure to die to his own self-centered desires.

Even though the husband's position as the head of the home is superior, their souls are equal. No husband must rule a wife as a king, but as a head that cares for and protects his body. The fact is, the woman was taken from the rib of man, the bone that was closest to his heart. Our attitude must be friendly, our language sweet, our commands sparing and respectful and our reproofs gentle. Love, not intimidation is the way to keep a wife. We husbands may pursue many tasks in life, but God reminds us: pursue love with your wife! After all, *"She is your companion and your wife by covenant,"* Malachi 2:14b NKJV. She is also our most important task.

95

## 2. God addresses wives.

Why did God specifically tell the wife to *"respect"* her husband? A wife generally has no problem loving her husband. She will cook, care for the kids, and even give her body to him sacrificially. But then, when she is with her friends her talk is disrespectful about her husband. This is really just self-pity, isn't it? In such a way, the wife is actually slapping the face of her husband in front of others. Does a body slap it's own head? She needs to, with respect, tell her husband and only her husband what is wrong, lovingly (Matthew 18:15). He is the one who can do something about it. A wife also shows respect when she does not seek to get in the last word, or say ten words to his one. A wife shows respect when she encourages her husband's headship instead of trying to steal it from him. A wife who is having a hard time respecting her husband needs to meditate on 1 Peter 2:18 to 1 Peter 3:6 and then begin to put it into practice.

### Silence shows more wisdom and respect than many words.

A gentle or quiet spirit in her heart shows more respect for his position, than gold on her face, (1 Peter 3:2-6). A husband will be more likely to change when the wife gives him respect. A wife who "respects" her husband will teach her children and others to follow her example. *"Then they can train the younger women to love their husbands and children,"* Titus 2:4. A wife is called to respect and love her man!

## 3. Love and respect in practice

A husband and wife will love and respect each other:
- When they confess their own sin to God and each other instead of to many other people.
- When they are not *"overcome by evil, but overcomes evil with good,"* Romans 12:21b NKJV.
- When they pray for each other.
- When they schedule their daily duties to honor God and to bless each other and their families.

- When they both do their daily duties for God's approval first, and to be a blessing to their spouse second.
- When they give praise to each other for their good qualities to encourage them in all their duties.
- When they express each others good points to others.
- When they seldom rebuke each other, but when they do it is private, quiet, sweet and short.

### A husband and wife cannot show "love" and "respect" unless they forgive each other!

We have already discussed this in chapter 8. It is briefly reviewed here. Never underestimate the power of forgiveness in keeping relationships strong. Keep in mind forgiveness is needed when we have been hurt in some way. If a husband waits to "love" his wife until she says, "I'm sorry," he is wrong. If the wife is bitter because the husband will not admit his wrong she is not forgiving him either. Waiting for the other to do some "good thing" before forgiveness or intimacy is granted is wages for work, not forgiveness. Basic Christianity is about forgiveness! We need to have it and we need to give it! We must "forgive each other just as in Christ God forgave you," Ephesians 4:32. God forgave us when we were dead sinners in Ephesians 2:5, and His enemies in Romans 5:10. When God forgave us He did three things and based on Ephesians 4:32, three things we must do.

1. After forgiving us, God never brings our sin against us again in person again. Thus, we must never bring up our spouse's sin against them in person again, once we have forgiven them.

2. When God forgive us, He never tells others about our sin. Thus, when we forgive someone we must not tell others either. If we do we have not really forgiven them as we are bringing it against them once again.

3. When God forgives us He never dwells on our sin anymore. When we forgive others, we must not dwell on it during the day or night. If we do, we are not only holding it against them, but we are harboring anger and bitterness, the opposite of forgiveness.

97

### Both husbands and wives

"*Submit to one another out of reverence for Christ,*" Ephesians 5:21. It is not only the wives who need to submit. The husbands also need to do so. Not only is this verse clear that all must "*submit to one another,*" but another verse sheds more light on the subject. "*Do nothing out of selfish ambition or vain conceit, but in humility consider others better than yourselves. Each of you should look not only to your own interests, but also to the interest of others,*" Philippians 2:3-4. We cannot be sincere about living the Christian life until we take these words to heart. How to do that is summarized next.

As husbands and wives, may we keep our eyes on the perfect example of the marriage relationship that exists between Christ and the church. May we humbly draw closer to the Head of that marriage, Jesus Christ. As we draw closer to Him in love and respect, we will in turn draw closer to each other. The Church and marriages have no greater need than to fall in love with Jesus. A wife who respects and loves Jesus and her husband will have a great marriage. A husband who loves and respects Jesus and his wife will have a great marriage! As our obedience to God's command to love, increases in our lives, so will God's grace and mercy also increase! May His kingdom come in our lives.

Some people are ready to give up on their marriages today and some are even thinking about divorce. Even though a loveless marriage is terrible, an anger-filled divorce will never be put behind you. Other couples refuse to consider divorce, which is good, but they live together as if they were divorced which is bad. Loveless marriages today are in the same deplorable condition as the Ephesian church that had lost its first love. Since Scripture clearly shows how the relationship between a man and a woman is the same picture as that of Christ and the Church, we will use Jesus' counsel to fix the following common example of a troubled marriage. Jesus knows how to bring back love and respect.

Using the Biblical pattern of love from 1 Corinthians 13:4-8a, finish these statements by making a list of failures of both husbands and wives to love their family.

People are not patient when they _____.

People are not kind when they _____.

People envy when they _____.

People boast when they _____.

People are proud when they _____.

People are rude when they _____.

People are self-seeking when they _____.

People are easily angered when they _____.

People keep a record of wrongs when they _____.

People delight in evil when they _____.

People do not protect when they _____.

People do not trust when they _____.

People do not persevere when they _____.

People fail when they _____.

# Introduction to Parenting

We need to love our children the way God intended us to. Keep in mind as we discuss many principles on parenting that the very same principles are also applicable to how we must lead in business, in the classroom, and in the church. The principles are the same because all four are discipleship relationships. It is always more profitable for us to study four things at once. Yet most of the examples we give will be for parents.

A most important parenting verse is: *"And you, fathers, do not provoke your children to wrath, but bring them up in the training and admonition of the Lord,"* Ephesians 6:4 NKJV. We focus on this verse because it leads us into the subject of loving leadership. From this verse we see it is a grievous sin on the part of a father or mother to provoke or tempt a child (or any other person) to sin. In another place Jesus said, *"Whoever causes one of these little ones who believe in Me to sin, it would be better for him if a millstone were hung around his neck, and he were drowned in the depth of the sea,"* Matthew 18:6NKJV.

Every disciple belongs to the Lord. God puts them in our life for the purpose of discipling them. Every one of us will be tested in The Judgment on how we brought up God's children! How arrogant and idolatrous it would be to bring up God's children, man's way! How damaging it would be to God's kingdom to go against His principles for living. How damaging to the disciple to be taught to live different from God's way of thinking. We must *"bring them up in the training and instruction of the Lord."* If we as Christian leaders fail to disciple God's way in the home, business, school and church, we miss the whole point of discipleship and we miss the whole point of the Great Commission.

How do we best prepare to be a leader in the home, church, school, or business? The best way is to, *"First, take the plank out of your own eye, and then you will see clearly to remove the speck from your brother's eye,"* Matthew 7:5b. God says the biggest problem for every leader is to first see the sin in their own life! If we are going to lead others through the minefield of problems in their life, we need clear vision. We need to take the log out of our eye. If we have a *"plank"* in our eyes, we cannot see a *"speck"* or *"sliver"* in another person! Notice God did not say there was a *"plank"* in their eyes. It is in ours. The question is: Are we taking the plank out of our eyes to be able to see clearly to help them?

When I teach about missions, I first use Matthew 7:1-5. Because how can anyone go out to pagans and say, "Jesus Christ changes lives," if He has not changed ours? There are two main ways we need to take the plank out of our eyes. First, the grace of God must be in and through us! "Grace" is not just a theological term. If we are taking the log out of our eye the grace of God will be very visible! Why? *"Out of the overflow of his heart his mouth speaks,"* Luke 6:45. When the grace of God changes hearts, people begin to act graciously! We cannot lead Biblically without grace!

Secondly, a parent also needs to know the process by which people change! Can you explain that process? Is not the biggest part of your discipling job in the home, church, school and business trying to get a disciple to change for the good? God outlines His process of change in Ephesians. With Christ and grace in us in Ephesians chapters 1-3, we now have the power to live differently! We can now put off the old nature or the old sin (Ephesians 4:22) and then replace it. Remember the word REPLACE. No disciple will change until he or she replaces the old wrong behavior and "puts-on" (Ephesians 4:24) the new pattern of living. But even then, change will still not occur until the new behavior is concentrated on! This is the Biblical process of all change.

*"Be imitators of God, therefore, as dearly loved children and live a life of love, just as Christ loved us and gave Himself up for us,"* Ephesians 5:1a. God clearly commands us to *"live a life of love,"* by *"being imitators of God."* How did God love us? God loved us by *"giving Himself"* freely to us. If you do not have grace in your heart, grace will never come out of you! Please, do not copy the many in

the church today who preach and teach much about the grace of God, but are as hard as nails in how they live. Such a person knows nothing about the grace of God! And this is not the kind of leader God calls us to be. Our walk must match our talk!

In the end, children need to live graciously also! "*Children, obey your parents in the Lord, for this is right,*" Ephesians 6:1. Remember the principle. All disciples need to obey, "for *this is right.*" One of the most important virtues in any child, worker, student or church member is obedience. God demands Biblical character in all of His children. Think about it. What if a disciple has the highest I.Q. in the world, but use their intelligence to lie, cheat, and steal? Is this a good disciple? No, of course not! Well, it is going to take grace on the part of the disciple to obey, and we need to encourage that grace by leading them in a gracious way!

Children, workers, students and church members not only need to obey but "*honor*" the one who is discipling them! "*Honor your father and mother which is the first commandment with a promise that it may go well with you and that you may enjoy long life on the earth,*" Ephesians 6:2-3. The problem is: All children are by nature inclined to "*honor*" self, not the one leading them. It will also take obedience and grace on every disciple's part to give "*honor.*" The disciple needs to know that there is a promise and a reward here if they are obedient in giving this "*honor.*" There is also a great reward for the leader who leads in a loving way to promote this honor and obedience in a disciple.

So, "*Fathers, do not provoke your children to wrath.*" God speaks here especially to "*fathers.*" But, this also applies to mothers as well since they are also spiritual leaders in the home. So how do we "*provoke our children to wrath*" and thus promote rebellion in them? And why did God single out wrath? Because "*wrath*" is the opposite of Biblical love! If we as leaders, manage and model our discipleship relationships with wrath, we are teaching wrong doctrine. Using "*wrath*" to lead is fear-based leadership. And it does work! But it is the world's way of leading, not God's!

"*Love one another*" is the echo of the Bible. Wrath does not love! James tells us, "*the wrath of man does not produce the righteousness of God,*" James 1:20. The point is, "*wrath*" in us promotes "*wrath*" in others! If you are trying to justify your "*wrath,*" you will find plenty of people who will agree, but God will not! God has clearly said, "*A man of great wrath will suffer punishment,*" Proverbs 19:9a. An angry woman drives a man (and children) out of the house in Proverbs 21:9 & 21:19. "*Wrath,*" is all about abusing power, not about leading by serving. So then, there are basically two ways to lead people. Just keep in mind that fear does motivate and lead! Every gangster, bully or terrorist knows this very well. However, God's way is a better way! Dr. John Stott has a great quote:

> "The authority by which the Christian leader leads is not power but love, not force but example, not coercion but reasoned persuasion. Leaders have power, but power is safe only in the hands of those who humble themselves to serve."

"*Love*" then is the test of every Christian life. For this reason, we are going to turn to the love chapter in the Bible to learn from God what our parenting and leadership skills should look like.

> "*Love is patient, love is kind. It does not envy, it does not boast, it is not proud. It is not rude, it is not self-seeking, it is not easily angered, it keeps no record of wrongs. Love does not delight in evil but rejoices with the truth. It always protects, always trust, always hopes, always perseveres. Love never fails,*" 1 Corinthians 13:4-8a.

# Chapter 1

# Parenting is Patient, Kind, and does not Envy

## 1. Parents provoke wrath when they are not "*patient.*"

As parents and leaders we live in a time in history when people want fast food, fast men, fast women, and fast everything else. We do not live in a *"patient"* world. If we are waiting for the world to teach *"patience"* to those we are responsible to disciple, forget it. It is something we must do every day by our own words and actions.

*"Patience"* is that calm rational spirit in how a person reacts or responds to evil persons and situations in his or her daily living. *"Patience"* is the grace of enduring the anger and injustice of others without being filled with resentment. *"Patience"* is the first loving virtue listed here in the love chapter that characterizes Biblical love. *"Patience"* is so important that without it, we will not have the peace of mind to put into practice the other parts of the love chapter.

Let this thought of a parent first having *"patience"* to be an effective leader sink in. Think of how 1 Corinthians 13:4-8 progresses in describing the attributes of a good, loving parent-leader. If we are not patient how will we be ever *"be kind"*? How can we stop *"envying,"* if we are not first *"patient"*? How can we stop our *"boasting"* if we are not first *"patient"*? How can we check our *"pride"* if we are not first *"patient"*? Neither will we be *"rude," "self-seeking,"* or *"easily angered"* if we are *"patient."* If we are going to teach *"patience"* to any disciple we need to live it first!

Being *"patient"* in life is really the same as saying we need a right attitude every day. James speaks clearly about how important a good attitude is saying, *"Count it all joy when you fall into various trials."* This wisdom is essentially about having a "patient attitude" in our day to day leadership responsibilities. This is where our daily trials are. Chuck Swindoll once said, "The older I get the more I realize that life is 10% what happens to me and 90% what my attitude is towards what happens to me." Patience and attitude is what makes up character, and character is what God wants in all of his disciples. *"Let patience have its perfect work, that you may be perfect and complete, lacking nothing,"* James 1:4.

"Am I *'patient'*?" is the question of the day? Can we pass the *"patience"* test of the Christian life? To understand how we are doing, we need to see clearly how we are "impatient."

- I am "impatient" when I care more about my needs, my rights and my agenda than I do about the needs of my child.
- I am "impatient" when I am not gracious or flexible to meet the needs of my disciple.
- I am "impatient" when I do not give my child time to change.
- I am "impatient" when I give them a task that is far beyond their capability to perform.
- I am "impatient" when I am rude. I am "impatient" when I am angry or bitter, refusing to forgive.

In the end, we have been impatient with those we have been called to lead! We have provoked our disciples to be filled with wrath with our lack of a *"patient"* spirit. We have hurt God's kingdom. May God forgive us! May He give His wisdom and power to live in a right way. May He give us His Spirit to follow the *"patience"* of Jesus Christ who was so meek and mild in His attitude!

### 2. Parents provoke wrath in others when they are not *"kind."*

*"Love is kind,"* 1 Corinthians 13:4b. Being *"kind"* to one another covers a wide range of how we treat each other. Being *"kind"* is to be sweet and gentle in the face of adversity. *"Kind"* is the same as being nice and the opposite of being nasty. Being *"kind"* is willingness to show respect and serve our children. Respect is the one thing that all people need in life! If a parent/leader is not willing to give respect to a disciple, that disciple will look for it elsewhere, even if it is with the rowdy group.

Being *"patient,"* and *"kind,"* are both building blocks of character. If there is one thing our modern world is short on, it's character.

How important is it really, if a person places 1st in their class in school, but lacks character? Is this the making of a good person? Personally, I would far rather hire someone of average intelligence with excellent character! Why? Because, if you hired a brilliant person and they did not have character they would use their cunning ability to cheat you! A *"patient"* and *"kind"* person would never seek to advance themselves by cheating others. Character is the need of the hour! A *"kind"* person would sacrificially protect you and others from outside dangers.

Women are by nature more patient and kind as they are more interested in relationships. A woman generally has a better idea on how to run a home calmly. For the man to take the lead in the home as God demands, he must get serious about relationships. A man must not be so driven to the task at hand that he does not see the needs of the children/disciple. Passages like 1 Timothy 3 and Titus 2 show how men need to be gentle and kind leaders in the home before they are even qualified to lead in the church. God is looking for character in leaders!

The modern world has put the obtaining of a college degree above the character qualifications. Is it any wonder we have leadership problems in so many homes, business, schools and churches. A *"kind"* leader not only to tells the truth but tells the truth with love. *"Kindness"* quietly and privately rebukes and corrects someone when they are wrong. *"Kindness"* is essential to get the job done without building resentment in others.

Jesus was the number one *"kind"* person ever! Jesus was so *"kind"* that it is said, *"He will not quarrel nor cry out, nor will anyone hear His voice in the streets. A bruised reed He will not break and a smoking flax He will not quench,"* Matthew 12:19-20a. How often do the neighbors hear our voices in the streets when we rebuke a child/disciple? How many bruised reeds (disciples) have we discouraged by our lack of kindness? How often have we snuffed out the fires of desire in our children by our cruel words?

- I "provoked my child to wrath" when I did not show "kindness" by disciplining them in front of others.
- I "provoked my disciple to wrath" when I gossiped about his/her problems to those not in a position to help.
- I was unkind to ignore the wrong behavior in a child/disciple.

In summary, our lack of kindness has worked to keep our children at arm's length. We have said things that we should not have said. We have said things that were correct, but without kindness. May God forgive us and help us to repair our relationships with Him and with those we are responsible to disciple. May we be more like Jesus who is so kind and loving to us, His children!

### 3. Parents provoke wrath in others when they are "envious."

"Love never is envious nor boils over with jealousy," The Amplified Bible. Because of "envy" a white girl in the USA lies in the sun to get brown. Because of "envy" a brown girl in India puts on powder and carries an umbrella to get whiter. Because of "envy," we secretly or openly want other people's social status, position of authority, money, clothes, and much more. Sinful "envy" is why we do this! "Envy" is ill will towards another, not love. My "envy" says God made a big mistake in not giving me this or that.

### "Envy" quickly leads to jealousy!

Envy quickly leads to jealousy, which in turn gossips by telling true stories to try defame or run down the character of others. Somehow we think this makes us more beautiful. It doesn't! Sure that beautiful girl in school has some faults but telling others about it is not very loving! Envy turns to jealously and also promotes the sin of slander by telling untrue stories to pull down the smart and efficient person advancing in the workplace. So, "envy" spreads both true and untrue stories to try pull others down.

A person who has an "envy" problem is really stealing. Just as a thief wants to steal a nice watch, our envy tells our mouth and fingers to take that which is not ours! As you can see, when evil envy leads to trying to deprive others, the sin becomes the greater. *"Love does not envy."*

### *"Envy"* sold a brother to the enemy.

Because of *"envy,"* the brothers of Joseph sold him into Egypt to get rid of him, Acts 7:9. Because of *"envy,"* the religious leaders of the Jewish community persecuted the church by hiring mobsters to trouble them, Acts 17:5. Because of *"envy"* church members, and leaders elbow for position today also. Because of *"envy"* David committed adultery with Bathsheba and murdered Uriah. *"Envy"* is evil because when we are preoccupied with getting "more," we are not content with what we have.

Our lust is *"envy"* and it will never be satisfied. True love is satisfied! *"Envy"* is called *"hateful"* in Titus 3:3, *"demonic"* in James 3:15 and indicates a depraved mind in Romans 1:29. We must first put off *"envy,"* to stop the fruit of it which is lying, cheating and stealing. *"Envy"* is a serious sin problem! *"Love does not envy."*

### Envy and jealousy drive us to fear and worry.

*"Envy"* and *"jealousy"* are key ingredients of fear, worry and depression! The reason is, *"envy"* is not thankful! *"Envy"* quickly gives in to self-pity and puts "Poor Me" on the throne. It is reported that 25% of college students are depressed. Talk to them and you will not find a thankful spirit. You will find a selfish, envious spirit that is basically lazy and undisciplined. *"Envy"* and *"Jealousy"* do not make a good attitude, and attitude leads to gratitude. *"Love does not envy."*

### Envy is rebellion and idolatry.

Grumbling and complaining are really *"envy"* and in the end it is rebellion against God. The Israelites had an *"envy"* problem and God scattered their bodies in the wilderness. *"Envy"* is idolatry because we think that we know more than God does about what we should have and what is best for us. We should not be surprised that *"envy"* is listed as a deed of the flesh in Galatians 5:19-21, and *"those who live like this will not inherit the kingdom of God."*

### "*Envy*" does not promote others.

"*Envy*" is particularly ugly in a leader because it does not seek to promote children, church members, students or workers. Why? Because the leader fears the disciple might somehow rise above them. It is a great tragedy that the great need of second level leadership everywhere, is lost because of an "*envious*" leader. How often I have seen this in business and in the church! Can you see why character is so critical in a leader?

### Because of our "*envy*," our children, workers, students and church members are greatly tempted to give-up.

When we do not notice the hard work of a disciple and reward it, they are tempted to give-up! And our own "*envy*" blinds us to the reality of this. We are so intent on being popular and advancing as a leader, that we just do not see the child, worker, student or church member crying. Did Jesus act like this? No, Jesus noticed the people. We can also, if we put off the sin of "*envy*."

### "*Envy*" breaks the 10ᵗʰ Commandment.

"*Thou shall not covet your neighbor's wife. You shall not set your desire on your neighbor's house or land, his manservant or maidservant, his ox or donkey, or anything that belongs to your neighbor.*" "*Envy*" not only breaks the 10ᵗʰ commandment but the other nine also. If we break one commandment, we brake them all. "*Love does not envy.*" May our God help us to understand that "*godliness with contentment is great gain.*"

# Chapter 2

# Parenting does not Boast, is not Proud, or Rude

## 1. Parents provoke wrath in others when they "boast"

*"Love does not boast,"* 1 Corinthians 13:4d. True love is more impressed with his or her unworthiness than his or her own merit. The Collins Dictionary describes boasting as, "to speak in excessively proud terms of one's possessions, skills or superior qualities." The whole purpose of leadership is to build up others. *"Boasting"* builds up self first, sees self as more important than anything. Biblical leadership practices sacrificial love where God is first and others are second. The Commandments teach this.

### A good parent/leader encourages and promotes.

Biblical discipleship is supposed to be concerned about ongoing leadership! A *"boastful"* leader will not take the time to even see the leadership potential in a disciple, let alone be concerned about the disciples of their disciples! Leadership of all kinds carries with it the absolute necessity to give encouragement! Would you not be tempted to be angry if your parent, business leader, teacher or pastor did not notice your abilities? What if your "leader" talked much about how great they were and how you did not measure up to them? You would be so frustrated that you might just shut-up, give-up and throw-up. If disciples stop trying, leaders should examine their own style of leadership.

Good leaders should not constantly compare one child to another by saying, "Why can't you be more like your brother or sister or me?" A good leader recognizes that people have different gifts and abilities. But, more than that, a good leader encourages them to use their gifts! Jesus noticed the weakest disciple, and then breathed new life into him. With His own blood, He bought His chosen of every tribe, language, people and nation.

### Take a "*boasting*" test.

Do you praise your spouse's accomplishments more, or your own? If your child gets good grades or someone has a good idea, do you take a little credit for it? If someone changes, do you talk more about how much time you put into this person or give the glory to God? How do you feel if you are treated like a servant?

King Nebuchadnezzar failed the boasting test saying, "*Is not this the great Babylon I have built as the royal residence, by my mighty power and for the glory of my majesty?*" "*The words were still on his lips*" Daniel 4:30-31a, when God made him like an animal for 7 years. After this Nebuchadnezzar finally "*raised his eyes to Heaven,*" (vs. 34) and God then restored him. He then said, "*Now I, Nebuchadnezzar, praise and exalt and glorify the King of Heaven, because everything He does is right and all His ways are just. And those who walk in pride He is able to humble,*" Daniel 4:37.

A "*boastful*" leader is insecure and is seldom willing to work with anyone that is older, has more education, or has more ability. A humble leader surrounds himself with good people, recognizes their abilities, encourages them to lead others. Is this not what discipleship is supposed to be? "*Love does not boast.*"

## 2. Parents provoke wrath in others when they are "*proud.*"

"*Love is not proud,*" 1 Corinthians 13:4e. The Bible clearly shows the seriousness of the sin of pride. "*Pride goes before destruction and a haughty spirit before a fall,*" Proverbs 16:18. "*The Lord will destroy the house of the proud,*" Proverbs 15:25a. "*The Lord detests all the proud of heart. Be sure of this: They will not go unpunished,*" Proverbs 16:5. God hates pride!

### What is so evil about pride?

God and others (in that order) are never first in a proud person's heart! "*In his pride the wicked does not seek Him, in all his thoughts there is no room for God,*" Psalm 10:4. Whether it is our looks, money, status, abilities or our spiritual growth it has been given to us by God alone. When we claim the glory for these, we are idolaters. God raised up every Christian "*to make the riches of His glory known...*"

116

*whom He prepared in advance for glory.*" So then, if God *"prepared in advance"* who we are and what we have, God deserves the thanks and praise, not us!

## Good leaders notice people.

The older I get the more I realize that successful leaders just plain notice people. A good leader notices his/her superiors, peers (equals), and those he or she is called to lead. A parent, business or school leader, or pastor who does not notice the people they are placed in authority over by saying "there are so many," or "I'm, so busy" does not deserve to be leading them.

What if we didn't look at our wife or child for three months? Things in our homes would be pretty bad if we played the ignore game! Then why do we do it in the business, school and in the church? The relationship is the same! The needs are the same! Not noticing a disciple has everything to do with whether or not they will follow us. Even if we think we do not need the love of a disciple, the disciple needs our love! When we do not notice those we lead, they are tempted to many sinful things including drugs. Then the parent complains, "My kid is so distant, I can't communicate with them."

## Start communicating!

Don't pick up a big hammer and hit them in the head! Start communicating by acknowledging our failure in the relationship! Talk about our mistakes and ask for the child/disciple's forgiveness. After all, we are told to take the log out of our own eye to see clearly to take the speck out of someone else's eye. Pride sees a speck in our eye and a log in the other's eye! Besides, a disciple saw our mistakes before we did. The point is: If we are confessors instead of professors we will have successors!

## Don't promote too quickly!

Ignoring a disciple is bad, but so is promoting them quickly. Granting privileges, before faithfulness is displayed, will spoil a child, student, worker, or church members and promote pride. God warns us not to put a *"recent convert"* into a leadership position in the church lest they *"become conceited and fall under the same judgment as the devil,"* in 1 Timothy 3:6. *"A man's pride brings him low, but the humble in spirit will retain honor,"* Proverbs 29:23. Our Lord clearly said, *"Blessed are the poor in spirit for theirs is the kingdom of Heaven."*

### 3. Parents provoke wrath in others when they are *"rude."*

Courtesy, tact and politeness are a display of love. *"Rude"* in the dictionary is insulting, discourteous, impolite, totally lacking refinement. As you can see the word *"rude"* covers a range of behaviors, that are not respectable or loving for a child of God. When a father is *"rude,"* to the mother, the children are learning how to be *"rude."* When a mother is disrespectful or *"rude"* to the father the children are learning how to be *"rude."* When a leader is *"rude"* to a worker he/she promotes rudeness to the customer.

### Abraham Lincoln has a great quote.

In referring to the proverb that tells us to bring up a child *"in the way he should go,"* Abraham Lincoln said it well. "There is just one way to bring up a child in the way he should go, and that is to travel that way yourself." We should not expect our male disciple to be a gentleman if we are displaying "rudeness" to them. We should not expect our female disciple to be sweet if we are bitter.

### Being "reverent" is the opposite of being "rude."

God created us to reverence Him, not to be *"rude"* to Him. *"Let us have grace, by which we may serve God acceptably with reverence and godly fear,"* Hebrews 12:28b. *"Godly fear"* is godly respect. We are called to reverence man also, who is created in the image of God. *"If anyone says 'I love God,' yet hates his brother he is a liar. For anyone who does not love his brother, who he has seen, cannot love God who he has not seen,"* 1 John 4:20.

*"Happy is the man who is always reverent,"* Proverbs 28:14a. We are not only to be *"reverent"* but *"always reverent."* Who are we *"always"* to be *"reverent"* to? When we greatly respect God and others we not only have reverence, but find true joy and peace in

118

the process. It is the Holy Spirit (God) who fills us with this joy, all because we are following God's loving and gracious commands (John 15:10-11). Obedience has rewards!

### God's guide to customer service.

*"Finally, all of you, live in harmony with one another; be sympathetic, love as brothers, be compassionate and humble. Do not repay evil with evil or insult with insult, but with blessing, because to this you were called so that you may inherit a blessing,"* 1 Peter 3:8-9.

*"Harmony,"* not "rudeness" is the way to customer service. *"Sympathetic"* reaches out to a customer, not "rudeness." *"Compassionate"* serves the customer well, not "rudeness." *"Humble"* not *"rude"* is the way to the heart of a customer as well as a disciple. If the customer *"insults"* you, *"bless"* him. In return and you will *"inherit a blessing"* in more ways than one!

From time to time, we need to rebuke or correct a disciple. That we do so is important. But it is just as important how we do it. Humble rebukes are quiet, in private, and rare. God comes to us alone, privately, very quietly, and we respect Him for that.

# Chapter 3

# Parenting is not Self-seeking, Angry, or Bitter

**1. Parents provoke wrath in others when they are *"self-seeking."***
Jesus summarized the Bible by telling us to love God first, and others second (Matthew 22:37- 40). Sad to say, many people in the church do not know this most basic theology. Recently, a professor in a Biblical denomination told me, "You have to love yourself more to come out of things like depression." What foolishness! Is this what Jesus had in mind about love? Did David in the Bible need to love himself more to get over his personal depression? No, he needed to love himself less and stop the adultery and murder! David needed to humble himself before God and confess his self-centered sin! Psalm 32 and 38 are clear. It is Satan who teaches you need to love yourself more! *"Everything in the world - the cravings of sinful man, the lust in his eyes and the boasting of what he has and does — comes not from the Father but from the world,"* 1 John 2:16.

### Does anyone even hate himself or herself?

Paul did not think so. He said, *"After all, no one ever hated his own body, but he feeds it and cares for it, just as Christ does the church,"* Ephesians 5:29. Not only do we love our own flesh/body we love it just as much as Jesus loves the Church, His body. Paul did not want us to even think it was even possible to hate our self.

It is psychology that teaches we need to love self more, to build up self, empower self, liberate self to solve our problems. You do not need to teach a baby, worker, student or church member to be *"self-seeking"* or to love self! They were all born that way! You will need to teach them the opposite. Loving self is the problem, not the solution! Loving self before God and others is not only idolatry but it is the main cause of anger, lust, adultery, drunkenness, fear and worry etc. Jesus said, *"If anyone would come after Me, he must deny himself and* take up his cross daily and follow Me. For whoever wants to save his life will lose it, but whoever loses his life for Me will save it. What good is it for a man to gain the whole world, and yet lose or forfeit his very self?'" Luke 9:23-25.

God warns: "But mark this: There will be terrible times in the last days. People will be lovers of themselves, lovers of money, boastful, proud, abusive, disobedient to their parents, ungrateful, unholy, without love, unforgiving, slanderous, without self-control, brutal, not lovers of the good, treacherous, rash, conceited, lovers of pleasure rather than lovers of God," 2 Timothy 3:1-4. We've arrived!

### Biblical love is the enemy of selfishness.

Love "seeketh not her own," KJV. Love is interested in others. Philippians 2:3-4 says, "Consider others better than yourself." The law of God demands this! Selfish people think much about their rights. Loving people think much about their responsibilities, and they listen! Which person would you like to have for a parent/leader or a disciple/worker? You are brain dead if you said you want a selfish person. Also, think more about how our ability to listen is really determined by our selfishness. We can't listen to others if we are into our self! One real test to see whether we are self-seeking is: Are we willing to listen to others?

### 2. Parents provoke wrath in others when they are "easily angered."

"Easily angered" does not need a definition. If we are "easily angered," we in turn provoke anger in a child, worker, student and church member. God is not talking about us being a little angry once in a while, but being "easily angered." Those "easily angered" have a temper and are no fun to be around! Love doesn't fly into a temper! Christian love does not get so exasperated because that is giving up, defeated. A loving leader keeps his or her head when everyone else loses theirs! A loving man or woman who masters their temper can master most anything.

122

### There is nothing righteous about *"anger."*

I am shocked on how many teach that anger often fits into the "righteous" category. God does not agree! He says, *"Man's anger does not bring about the righteous life that God desires,"* James 1:20. In our pride and blindness we try make excuses for our anger. We say we get over it quickly, so then it's okay. We say that we were born like that. We say Jesus was angry so we can be angry too. All are lies, because it says someone else is the problem!

### Where does *"anger"* come from?

Herein lies one of the greatest questions ever! If a parent/leader does not even know the real cause of anger in his or her own life and how to overcome it, how will they ever teach others how to overcome it? If we claim, "this or that person made me angry," that too is a lie! Anger never comes from someone else! Oh sure, others tempt us to be angry, but that is much different than the cause of it. God tells us the cause. *"But the things that come out of the mouth come from the heart, and these make a man unclean,"* Matthew 15:18.

Luke didn't doubt the source of our evil anger either! *"The good man brings good things out of the good stored up in his heart, and the evil man brings evil things out of the evil stored up in his heart. For out of the overflow of his heart his mouth speaks,"* Luke 6:45.

### *"Easily angered"* people end up in hell if they don't change.

The deeds of the flesh shout to us about the evil of being *"easily angered"* as we see eight different sinful habits that are connected to anger! All eight are listed along with *"murder," "adultery," "idolatry"* and *"drunkenness."* The 8 are: *"hatred, discord, jealousy, fits of rage, selfish ambition, dissensions factions, and envy."* And then God goes on to say, *"I warn you, as I did before, that those who live like this will not inherit the kingdom of God,"* Galatians 5:19-21. The KJV reads, *"Those who practice such things will not inherit the kingdom of God."* If we are *"easily angered"* we will be known by the *"practice"* of it. Then God says, *"Those who live like this will not inherit the kingdom of God."* Anger is seriously wrong!

In Proverbs 29:22 we read, *"An angry man stirs up dissension, and a hot-tempered one commits many sins."* But do not think only a man has this problem! *"Better to live on the corner of a roof than share a house with a quarrelsome wife,"* Proverbs 21:9. A angry parent/leader *"provokes"* others to be angry also. If God's grace has really changed us, then grace is in our hearts and we are not *"easily angered."* James gives us the replacement for anger. *"My dear brothers, take note of this: Everyone should be quick to listen, slow to speak and slow to become angry,"* James 1:19.

### 3. Parents provoke wrath in a child when we *"keep a record of wrongs."*

We keep a record of wrongs when we focus intently on a child's failures, without noticing their talents. If you want a child, student, worker or church member to lose hope, just keep telling them about their faults without ever noticing their good points! This is a serious mistake! Can you live without encouragement?

### Keeping a *"record of wrongs,"* is essentially bitterness.

When a disciple experiences mostly criticism, anger is provoked in them because that is what is shown to them! Keeping a *"record of wrongs,"* is bitterness! Our Lord shows us how damaging bitterness is to our own personal lives, *"Pursue peace with all men, and holiness, without which no one will see the Lord: looking diligently lest anyone fall short of the grace of God; lest any root of bitterness spring up cause trouble, and by this many become defiled,"* Hebrews 12:14 NKJV. 1. A *"bitter"* person will not *"see the Lord."* 2. Bitterness falls short of God's grace. 3. "Bitterness" causes trouble with many! 4. Bitterness defiles many. Bitterness is serious!

### Bitterness is *"demonic."*

*"But if you harbor bitter envy and selfish ambition in your hearts, do not boast about it or deny the truth. Such 'wisdom' does not come down from heaven but is earthly, unspiritual, of the devil. For where you have envy and selfish ambition, there you find disorder and every evil practice,"* James 3:14-16. Bitterness is called here in the NIV "of

*the devil"* but the NKJV renders it *"demonic."* Demons provoke wrath in others, never peace and love.

### Forgiveness is the Biblical replacement for bitterness.

Nothing promotes relationships more than putting off bitterness and putting on forgiveness. Nothing! Forgiveness is the oil for the engine, the train track for the train. Without forgiveness, relationships with God and man go nowhere. *"We must forgive just as God in Christ has forgiven us,"* Ephesians 4:32. *"In Christ,"* God *"remembers our sin "against us no more"* (Ezekiel 18:22, Psalm 32:2). Forgiveness means three things for us. When God forgives us, He doesn't ever bring up our sin *"against us"* again: 1. Not to our face personally, 2. Doesn't tell others, and 3. Doesn't dwell on it Himself. Because of Ephesians 4:32, we are to do the same!

### How else did God forgive us?

When God forgave us, He put our sin *"behind His back,"* Isaiah 38:17b. God forgave us *"while we were His enemies,"* in Romans 5:10; While we were *"dead"* in Ephesians 2:1: While we were *"dead"* and *"sinning"* in Ephesians 2:5. In grace God gave us what we needed, not what we deserved! Because we were recipients of grace we must now give mercy and grace to "our disciples" when it is not deserved! If we expect others to prove their love to us before we will show them grace and love, then we are *"keeping a record of wrongs,"* and know nothing about forgiveness. Such an evil attitude demands perfection in others, before acceptance by us.

We must forgive anyone and everyone. Jesus said, *"When you stand praying, if you hold anything against anyone, forgive him, so that your Father in Heaven may forgive your sins,"* Mark 11:25.

# Chapter 4

# Parenting does not Delight in Evil, but Rejoices with the Truth, Protects, and Trusts

**1. Parents provoke wrath in others when they *"delight in evil."***

To *"delight in evil"* is to be enslaved to any sinful act without turning from it. So, if we love a sin more than we love God, we *"delight in evil."* Leaders in the home, church, school and business actually push people away from God if they teach one way, and live another. It is the way we live, not the degrees behind our name that is the primary requirement to be in ministry (1 Timothy 3). And all life is ministry for the Christian.

- An employer *"delights in evil"* when he is addicted to gambling, drinking, anger and the deeds of the flesh, in Galatians 5:19-21.
- A father *"delights in evil"* when he proudly tells stories of his sinful past.
- A leader *"delights in evil"* when he neglects to read the Bible and prays for those he is leading.
- A wife *"delights in evil"* when she gossips about her family to others who do not have a reason to know.
- A husband *"delights in evil"* by demanding that his family keep the family name "pure," while he embraces a lust problem.
- A teacher *"delights in evil"* when she demands the children are prepared for class when she is not.
- A business leader *"delights in evil"* when he/she takes a bribe and then tells the workers not to cheat or steal.
- A pastor *"delights in evil"* when he demands that the people re-pent when he is not working on repentance in his own life.
- *"If a ruler* (leader) *pays attention to lies, all his servants* (disciples) *become wicked,"* Proverbs 29:12.

- If a leader approves of, or rewards evil things to advance a disciple's position, (even laughing at naughty children) then we "reward evil for good" and "evil will not depart from his house," Proverbs 17:13.
- We specifically "delight in evil," when "we call evil good and good evil," Isaiah 5:20. To such, God says: "Woe unto them."

## 2. Parents provoke wrath in others when they do not "rejoice with the truth."

In the process of change, "delighting in evil" in the last lesson, was what we needed to put off. That process is never complete until we replace it with the put-on "rejoice with the truth." If we are not "rejoicing with the truth" there are two possible problems. One, we are not confessing the evil we delighted in as sin or we are not forsaking it. Two, we are not planning the new right behavior we must put-on to replace the old, and then concentrating on it.

A joyful Christian is excited daily about his or her faith. Think of what the word "rejoice" really means. It is to have joy over and over again. Joy is not the same as laughter. Joy again and again, is the comfort of knowing that we are God's redeemed children forever. It is possible to have joy in the midst of sorrow. Lasting joy is first in the Lord, and then in others. We find misery, after a very short joy, when we serve ourselves first in our adultery, drunkenness, anger, etc...

To "rejoice in the truth," we need to know "the truth"!!! One of the greatest problems in the church worldwide is that many people know about the Truth (Jesus), but they do not know The Truth - personally that is. Jesus must be the most important Person in our life to "rejoice in the truth." Do you have a relationship with Him?

To "rejoice in the truth" we also need to live "the truth." To live "the truth" we need to keep the commandments. Many people know about the commandments and the truth, but live a lie. Children, workers, students and church members are all frustrated and greatly provoked when those in leadership say they believe one thing and do another. We only believe what we practice. If we say we do not believe in adultery, but then commit adultery, we believe in adultery. Hypocrites do not make good leaders.

Jesus said, *"If you obey my commands, you will remain in my love, just as I have obeyed my Father's commands and remain in His love. I have told you this so that My joy may be in you and that your joy may be complete,"* John 15:10-11. The Holy Spirit gives us this joy, after we are in Christ, after we are obedient, John 14:15-16.

How often we have pursued the short-lived joy of sin. How often we have also lost our joy because we have put our hope in others changing, instead of treating them with love, and waiting for You to change them. We have not known much about the meaning of *"rejoice,"* because we have not looked to find our joy in God first. May we experience *"rejoicing"* in God's truth that sets us free!

### 3. Parents provoke wrath in children when they fail to *"protect."*

Love *"protects."* When a mother hen sees danger, she immediately spreads her wings to *"protect"* her chicks. When a loving shepherd sees danger, he or she *"protects"* the sheep. David, the shepherd boy, killed a lion and a bear with his hands to protect the sheep. As leaders, do we see the "lions" and "bears" that are waiting to grab those we are responsible to lead? Are we protecting them?

How God *"protects"* us is the best example. God in trinity works in unity to *"protect"* us in salvation (Ephesians 1), and in sanctification. Do we have this kind of unity in our homes, businesses, schools and churches? If not, why not? If the grace of God is in us, then this same grace must flow out of us to others!

Let us review the love chapter we have been studying. Let us see how love *"protects"* us, and those we are called to lead. We first looked at patience, and then added kindness, two graces we must put-on. Then we saw a complete lack of love or grace in envy, boasting, pride, rudeness, self-seeking, anger, bitterness and delighting in evil. If we put off these sins that are so lacking of grace and replace them with *"rejoicing in the truth,"* we would be protecting those we are called to lead.

As leaders, we have a responsibility to *"protect"* as our head protects our body. God placed our physical heads high on top of our shoulders, above everything else. Four of our five senses are located in our head, specifically to *"protect"* our body. Our eyes see danger! Our ears listen for danger! Our mouth speaks of danger! Our nose smells danger! All of these senses are designed to *"protect"* our body.

- When we seldom open the Word of God, we do not *"protect"* those we are called to lead! If *"the fear of the Lord is the beginning of wisdom,"* then it is about time we start reading it so that we can become a wise leader.
- We have failed to *"protect"* our children by freely allowing the T.V. to openly display shame and bad language.
- We have failed to *"protect"* our children by allowing them to dress as the world dresses and basically expose themselves.
- When a parent, businessman, teacher or pastor is enslaved to lust and adultery, they can only follow not lead. In such a way they do not *"protect"* their children.
- When a leader in business cheats and steals to get ahead, he/she does not *"protect"* the workers, but encourages followers to do the same.
- When a husband or father does not cultivate a close relationship with his wife or daughter who needs much affection, he does not *"protect"* them and they are tempted to look elsewhere to find it.
- When a mother does not teach her son to be gentle, will he learn how to be a gentleman, and thus *"protect"* him from being abusive?
- A leader in the home, business, school and church does not *"protect"* a disciple if they gossiped about them or slandered them! *"Whoever secretly slanders his neighbor, him I will destroy,"* Psalm 101:5a.
- A leader's prayers will go unanswered if they *"keep sin in their hearts"* based on Psalm 66:18 and 1 Peter 3:7.

In summary, we have not seriously protected those whom we are supposed to keep from evil. May God be merciful to us sinners and help us to lovingly *"protect"* those we are leading!

## 4. Parents provoke wrath in children when they do not *"trust."*

Love *"always trust"* is the NIV reading. The word *"trust"* gives the meaning of having a complete confidence in someone. To be effective a leader in the home, business, school, or church must *"trust"* in two main ways to be effective.

### First, we must trust fully in God.

God is perfect in knowledge, perfect in power, perfectly holy, and perfectly everywhere at once. Thus, we can *"trust"* Him to have the ability to keep His promises and be true to His Word. *"Trust"* and faith go hand in hand. If we do not have a close relational *"trust"* in God, we will be operating in our own strength which ends in fear and worry. *"Trust in the Lord with all your heart and lean not on your own understanding; in all your ways acknowledge Him and He will make your paths straight,"* Proverbs 3:5-6.

### Secondly, we must develop *"trust"* in others.

This necessary "trust" in others takes on many different forms. The objective of leadership is to raise up a new generation of good leaders in the home, business, school and church. If we do not trust in others to help share in the leadership load, then we will not delegate responsibilities! If we fail to delegate responsibilities, not only will nothing get done but we will also not have second level leadership. All the while we are complaining and then burn out from the strain.

### Three people who refused to *"trust."*

I recently met with two students and an older man who had severe "trust" problems. Basically they were stressed out, nervous wrecks who would not focus on their daily duties, and would not sleep without pills at night. The main reason for their struggle was twofold.

In the daytime, they refused to *"trust"* Christ and leave their burdens at the Cross. So they dragged their problems around like a prisoner chained to a heavy ball. They also refused to seek advice from others who could share their burden.

In the nighttime, they once again refused to leave their burdens at the Cross and *"trust"* Christ, to make their "paths straight." Instead, their many burdens circled in their mind like an airplane that circles an airport. They would rather carry around their own problem than take them to the Cross of Christ. Why don't they go there? They don't trust Christ. So then their problem is really sinful fear and worry.

## What is wrong with fear and worry?

Jesus called worry, *"little faith"* in Matthew 6:30b. Jesus called fear "wicked and lazy" in Matthew 25:25-26. Not only that, Jesus sent the one who was "afraid" straight to hell in Matthew 25:30 for a lack of a trusting faith. The problem is what do we call fear and worry since they are key components to a lack of *"trust."* Do we agree with Jesus or do we think this is some small innocent problem?

You have just seen two reasons a lack of trust is so wrong! A lack of *"trust"* is wrong because it leads to fear about the things that went wrong in the past, and worry that it might happen again in the future, consequently, we do NOTHING in the present. Furthermore, even in the midst of our inactivity, we are burning out from the entire struggle mentally and spiritually.

When a Christian is said to be struggling, do you know what his or her basic problem is? Struggling is really just plain delayed obedience and a lack of fully trusting God. The old song is correct, "Trust and obey for there is no other way to be happy in Jesus than to trust and obey." So important is "trust" in a believer's life. Satan loves it when we are inactive from a lack of trust, for then, we lack the motivation to work for God's kingdom. Psalm 37 shows us we cannot put on "trusting in the Lord", and "delighting in the Lord," and "resting in the Lord," until we first put off "envying" what others have. May God help us who are weak and have not trusted our God as we should!

# Chapter 5

# Parenting Hopes, Perseveres, and Never Fails

**1. Parents provoke wrath in children when they fail to give _"hope."_**
People can't live without _"hope."_ When people come in for counsel and need help in their life, the one thing that they lack is _"hope."_ But, we must not give people the world's kind of hope. The world's hope is nothing but a wish, since it is dependent on the need for people, possessions or circumstances to change. The "hope" a Christian has is not dependent on created things of any kind, but on the Creator of everything. A Christian's _"hope"_ is in God the Father, God's Son, and God's Spirit. A Christian's _"hope"_ is in God's Word and trusting in His ability to keep His promises.

### _"Hope deferred makes the heart sick,"_ Proverbs 13:12.

People without _"hope"_ get sick! The question of the day is: Do we give _"hope"_ in our discipleship relationships, or do we steal the little _"hope"_ that they have by our silence or neglect? Our criticism, without the balance of encouragement, really steals _"hope."_ Actually, if we are overly critical, we ourselves lack "hope"!

### We lose _"hope"_ because we neglect to pray.

We are tempted, not caused, to lose _"hope"_ when someone in our life just will not change. If our _"hope"_ remains in God to change people, then we will wait for God to change people, while we continue to love them, even when they treat us like dirt. If we do not understand that only God can change a human heart, and keep our eyes on Him, then we will try many weird things to change people, and be upset when they don't.

Apart from a changed heart from the Lord, we cannot have, or give, _"hope."_ Job in the Bible had _"hope"_ because he trusted in the goodness and mercy of God! Have our disciples learned to trust in

God first? Or, have they learned to trust more in various created things like money, health, reputation, etc... before trusting in God? In great difficulties, Job could say *"I know that my redeemer liveth."* Job said, *"In my flesh I shall see God."* Job had hope! Do you have this hope? May we hope in the One who *"always works all things for our good,"* Romans 8:28.

## 2. Parents provoke wrath, when they do not *"always persevere."*

*"Love perseveres."* Love causes us not to give up on the ones we are discipling. Love can bear insult, injury or disappointment. To *"persevere"* in love, is to continue with a loving attitude regardless of the circumstances in life. We just studied *"hope,"* without this no one will ever have the eyes to *"persevere."* To *"persevere"* in life is keeping our eye on the main goal, faithfulness, not happiness or money!

We are tempted to switch from faithfulness to worrying about results or consequences. Results are God's responsibility! God calls our worry *"little faith"* in Matthew 6:30b. A leader who gives in to worry is little in faithfulness, spinning his or her wheels, not keeping their eye on the goal.

A leader in the home, business, school or church who has a fear problem will never *"persevere"* in love either! In fact, it takes *"perfect love"* to *"cast out fear,"* 1 John 4:18. Jesus was so concerned about fear that in Matthew 25:14-30, He tells a parable to emphasize it. Three men were stewards and the Master (Jesus) left them and went on a long journey (to Heaven). At the end of the lives of the three men they stood before the Master in The Judgment. To the first two stewards Jesus said, *"Well done, good and faithful servant!"* To the third Jesus said, *"You wicked and lazy servant,"* Matthew 25:26. Why? The third man said he could not be faithful because he was afraid.

It would not be so bad if we feared and worried for one day. But the problem is, we do it again the next day and then the next until it becomes a lifelong pattern. A leader that manages his or her life like this is wicked and lazy because they do not *"persevere."* The man in the parable who was called *"wicked and lazy,"* by Jesus was told to be thrown "*outside, into the darkness, where there will be weeping and gnashing of teeth*," Matthew 25:30. He was actually sent to hell!

To "*always persevere*" means to, "*Stand firm. Let nothing move you. Always give yourselves fully to the work of the Lord*," because "*you know that your labor in the Lord is not in vain*," 1Corinthians 15:58b. What does it mean to give "*yourselves fully to the work of the Lord*"? It simply means we need to "*persevere*" in loving God and others. And that too is the perfect love that cast out fear.

Actually, it is God who "*perseveres*" us in the Christian life. That is why we need to keep our eyes on Him. Even when we sin, God, in love, convicts us by His Holy Spirit, giving us guilt, John 16:7-8. With our heavy guilt we go to the Cross, confessing our sin. Praise God, He drives us there. The big question is: Are we going to the Cross with our concerns or are we in fear and worry, drowning in self-centered contemplation? Can you now see how fear and worry is "*wicked*," "*lazy*," and "*little faith*"?

God "*perseveres*" us even more when He forgives our sin. We persevere even more yet when we likewise "*forgive others just as God in Christ has forgiven us*." The whole process of reconciliation, whereby we confess our sin, ask for forgiveness, and then promise to repent, and then go concentrate on new righteous behavior is in a nutshell how we "*persevere*." The number one way we fail to "*persevere*" is when we to fail to listen to the prompting of the Holy Spirit and start this process of confessing our sin, in specific detail. "*Perseverance*" then is repeating that process, again and again when we fail. And we will fail.

To "*persevere*," we need to "*overcome evil with good*," Romans 12:21b. We need to think, "*I can do everything through Him who gives me strength*," Philippians 4:13a. With a positive, overcoming, faithful, forgiving spirit that is locked in on the Cross of Christ, we will "*persevere*." In Revelation 21:8 those who "*overcome*" inherit Heaven. In Revelations 21:9, "*Cowards*," are listed first among those who will be in hell. May we "*persevere*" and then teach others to do the same!

### 3. Parents provoke wrath when they *"fail."*

*"Love never fails."* The context of 1 Corinthians chapters 12-14 is spiritual gifts. All gifts fail without *"faith, hope and love."* *"But the greatest of these is love,"* 1 Corinthians 13:13. Love is most important! Love was clearly described for us in the love chapter so that we may be fully convinced that it is these specific parts of our character that need to be developed and displayed. This is what makes us a loving person! If you and I *"fail"* in love, we *"fail"* as leaders. If we *"fail"* as leaders, how can we disciple anyone?

### God's love never fail us.

We can understand our "love failures" by seeing how God's love never fails us. What is there about the love of God that never fails His adopted, chosen children? Actually there are a few important steps whereby God loves us.

### First, God planned to love us.

God loved us even before we were created or made. *"For He chose us in Him before the creation of the world to be holy and blameless in his sight,"* Ephesians 1:4. Sometime we plan not to like someone even before we get to know them! Do we plan our love for others?

### Second, God planned for us *"to be holy and blameless."*

Is it our plan for our children, workers, students and church members to be *"holy and blameless"*? Is this our prayer before our children are even conceived? Is this our prayer before we hire a worker? Is this our concern even before we teach a student? Is it our hope that each new church member will be *"holy and blameless in His sight"*? God chose us to be "holy" when we were ugly with sin!

### *"Never will I leave you; never will I forsake you,"* Hebrews 13:5.

God does not leave us when we sin! As Christians, He forgave us from all of our sins, while we were His enemies (Romans 5:10). God continues to give us daily forgiveness. Does our love for others clear them of the past and reach out to them daily? If not, our love *"fails."*

138

"Who shall separate us from the love of Christ?" Romans 8:35a. Can "tribulation, or distress, or persecution" separate us from those we are discipling? If it can, then our love "fails." "No created thing, shall be able to separate us from the love of God," Romans 8:39b. Is another relationship or even money, (created things) separating us from others? If so, our love "fails." "The Lord disciplines those whom He loves," Hebrews 12:6a. Do we discipline those we love? If we do not our love, "fails." Or, do we expect complete obedience from others, and if it is not there, we reject them?

Loving, Biblical leadership "never fails." A real Biblical "leader" understands that discipling others is all about lovingly teaching, rebuking, correcting, and training them to remain faithful, following the outline of 2 Timothy 3:16-17. If we add up all of our failures, we have been selfish and preoccupied with serving ourselves instead of serving God and others.

# Chapter 6

# The Leadership Skills Jesus Learned

Jesus learned many discipleship skills before He began the ministry. In fact, Jesus had 30 years of leadership training. Too often this somewhat silent period of Jesus' life is overlooked. We will look more closely at what Jesus learned, to test us to see if we are teaching these same things to others.

Starting as a two-year-old, all Hebrew children needed to learn and recite daily the following verses called the "Shema," which follows the giving of the 10 commandments:

*"Hear, O Israel: The Lord our God, the Lord is one. Love the Lord your God with all your heart and with all your soul and with all your strength. These commandments that I give you today are to be upon your hearts. Impress them on your children. Talk about them when you sit at home and when you walk along the road, when you lie down and when your get up. Tie them as symbols on your hands and bind them on your foreheads. Write them on the doorframes of your houses and on your gates,"* Deuteronomy 6:4-9.

### The following observations can be made.

Leadership is about obedience. Hearing about doing right is not enough. Leaders must do right. Doing right is to be *"upon their hearts."* Leaders need a holy reverence for the commandments, which in part teach the following: respect for those in authority, don't lie, don't cheat, don't steal, don't commit adultery, and don't covet. Jewish fathers kissed the commands of God when they entered their houses. Jesus observed and did all this.

Leadership is about relationships. A leader who has more interest in his or her own personal goals instead of the follower's progress, is inclined to "privileged leadership" instead of "sacrificial servanthood." Thus, leaders are to be with those they are leading. Absent leaders who say they spend "quality time," as a substitute for much time, are not giving of their time in God's way. Leaders are to "sit" and "walk" with those they were leading. Leadership is not all about group meetings! It has more to do with individual attention! A single most important trait of Jesus is that He was with His disciples.

- As a young carpenter, Jesus learned how to work. Jesus knew the importance and the satisfaction of hard, sacrificial, physical work for the benefit of others. Today, too many want to be leaders, even in the church, because they are too lazy to work.

- As a young carpenter, Jesus learned how to establish working relationships to accomplish a common goal. Too many leaders today selfishly use manipulation to advance their own kingdom.

- As a young carpenter, Jesus learned about the work process. He learned how to take wood, steel and stone from the rough original shape, and mold it into a finished product for the customer. Using the same process, Jesus took "rough fishermen," and shaped them into vessels for the King.

- As a young carpenter, Jesus learned the importance of character. Today, many leaders know much about books but little of character. As a result many leaders have knowledge without much wisdom. And then, because of some degree want to be some kind of royalty without much loyalty.

- As a young carpenter, Jesus learned how to manage. He had a product, His time, and limited resources. With these He learned to schedule, budget, prioritize and constantly evaluate. Later on with His disciples, Jesus had a tight schedule (3 years), a limited budget (a stone for a pillow and little food to feed many). He prioritized events to teach the right things in the right order. He constantly evaluated His disciples using a gentle rebuke and steady encouragement with much love.

- As a young carpenter, Jesus was given opportunity to display His skills and delegate responsibilities to others. Today many leaders hang on to absolute control like a child does with a chocolate. Jesus knew the process of discipleship multiplication and used it. Many leaders pretend much about their followers "developing their gifts," but know little about encouraging or allowing them to use those gifts.

May we not learn leadership ideas on how to disciple from the world instead of from our Lord. For He is the Way, the Truth and the Life. His  methods of leadership are timeless and priceless. Unlike Jesus, we have wrongly favored educational advancement over character development. We have not followed His example. We have been more interested in self-advancement than in advancing those we are discipling. May God forgive us for not working on relationships in our lives. May we spend more time with our disciples, edifying them. May God implant in our hearts the strong desire to glorify Him in everything that we do. May He guide us to follow His pattern of leadership!

# Chapter 7

# What is Biblical Discipline?

*"God disciplines us for our good that we may share in His holiness. No discipline seems pleasant at the time, but painful. Later on, however, it produces a harvest of righteousness and peace for those who have been trained by it,"* Hebrews 2:10-11.

We can see from the following verse that discipline is "good"!

*"God disciplines us for our good that we may share in His holiness. No discipline seems pleasant at the time, but painful. Later on, however, it produces a harvest of righteousness and peace for those who have been trained by it,"* Hebrews 2:10-11.

God wants us to *"share in His holiness."* That is a pretty good reason to desire the discipline of God for our own lives. It is also a good reason to discipline those we are called to disciple. After all, *"holiness"* makes a much better child, worker, student and church member. Surely we would all agree that *"holy"* is better than having a liar, cheater and one who steals as our disciple.

### The word discipline is part of the word disciple.

Everyone is involved in different discipleship relationships in their life. We disciple in the home, in business, in school and in the church. So then, it is not a question on whether or not we will disciple or discipline, but whose wisdom should we use to do it? Should we use the world's way or God's way? Since every disciple belongs to God first, and *"The fear of the Lord is the beginning of knowledge,"* Proverbs 1:7, we should follow God.

### The Scriptures show us what discipline does.

*"All Scripture is God-breathed and is useful for teaching, rebuking, correcting and training in righteousness, so that the man of God may be thoroughly equipped for every good work,"* 2 Timothy 3:16-17.

What we have here is a four-step process to reach the goal of a disciple that is to  be *"trained in righteousness."*

### Every house needs God's laws to run smoothly.

Every household needs good, clear rules to function well. Without rules, there is chaos. But, what are the best rules? How many rules should there be in a home? What happens when someone breaks the rules? God gives us ten simple, loving rules in Exodus 20 and Deuteronomy 5.

### God's rules for our home

1. **You shall have no other god's before Me.**
2. **No idols must be made or worshiped.**
3. **You shall not misuse the name of the Lord your God.**
4. **Remember the Sabbath day by keeping it holy.**
5. **Honor your father and your mother.**
6. **You shall not murder.**
7. **You shall not commit adultery.**
8. **You shall not steal.**
9. **You shall not lie against anyone or about anything.**
10. **You shall not covet what others have.**

### The importance of obeying God's rules.

After God gave these commands to man, He said, *"So be careful to do what the Lord your God has commanded you; do not turn aside to the right or to the left. Walk in all the way that the Lord your God has commanded you, so that you may live and prosper and prolong your days,"* Deuteronomy 5:32-33a. God went on to say, *"These commands that I give you today are to be upon your hearts. Impress them on your children. Talk about them when you sit at home and when you walk along the road, when you lie down and when you get up. Tie them as symbols on your hands and bind them on your foreheads. Write them on the doorframes of your houses and on your gates,"* Deuteronomy 6: 6-9. In fact, the whole Bible is a command to love. Are there any rules more important than God's rules?

### Grace must also govern the home.

Be careful. Do not use the law of God like it is a hammer! Why? Because even though God's laws must guide the home, His grace must govern it also. If a parent teaches the law of God in a spirit of anger, then he or she is not teaching God's way. God gave us His law because He loved us and knew this was the best way to guide us. Law without love is more like abuse. *"If I have not love, I am only a resounding gong or a clanging symbol,"* 1 Corinthians 13:1b.

God is not a mean, angry dictator. He is a loving God. His justice and His love are more equally balanced than a scale at the vegetable market. If love and justice are not equally balanced in our home, we will cheat God and our children!

### Permissiveness is not the strategy of the Scriptures.

Since *"folly is bound up in the heart of a child,"* Proverbs 22:15a, letting them do what they naturally want to do will be their destruction. The verse, *"Train a child in the way he should go, and when he is old he will not turn from it,"* Proverbs 22:6 is quoted by many people as a promise in a very wrong way. Bruce A. Ray in his excellent book, "Withhold Not Correction" says:

> "In its proper context, Proverbs 22:6 is not a promise so much as it is a warning to Christian parents. In the Hebrew text of Proverbs 22:6, the phrase *'in the way he should go,'* is entirely lacking. Rather the Hebrew says, 'Train up a child in his way and when he is old he will not depart from it.'"

> *"God disciplines us for our good that we may share in His holiness. No discipline seems pleasant at the time, but painful. Later on, however, it produces a harvest of righteousness and peace for those who have been trained by it,"* Hebrews 2:10-11.

## Jay Adams also comments on Proverbs 22:6 in his book "Competent to Counsel."

"This verse stands not as a promise but as a warning to parents that if they allow a child to train himself after his own wishes (permissively) they should not expect him to want to change these patterns when he matures. Children are born sinners and when allowed to follow their own wishes, they will naturally develop sinful habit responses. The basic thought is that such habit patterns become deep seated when they have been ingrained in the child from earliest days."

### A little tree is easily bent.

So then, it is our job as parents to train the child to live God's way! It is easy to bend a tree straight when it is yet a little sapling, but to straighten it when it is full grown cannot even be done with a team of horses. The longer bad habits get ingrained, generally, the longer it will take to implement new Biblical ones. This is also true in business, in the church, and in the school also. If you see a problem and ignore it, the situation will get worse not better! "If it isn't broke don't fix it," is not a Biblical proverb! We need to fix discipline problems when they first appear. God gives a picture of a lion to Cain in Genesis 4:7, when He said *"sin is crouching at your door."* The word *"flee"* is used in 2 Timothy 2:22 to show us urgency concerning sin. Waiting is the devil's plan!

### Hazards to discipline

Often parents with children who are hooked on drugs, pornography and other evils wring their hands, crying, "What can I do?" Let us look at a common situation and see if this fits you? Often pastor's children are the most rebellious of all children. Why is this? Too often these children see a big difference between the life of the father lived on Sunday in church from his lived the rest of the week. The pastor preaches from the pulpit, "You need to repent. You need to confess your sins to God and to the ones in your life you have sinned against." His children hear this sitting in the church and think:

148

"When have you ever confessed anything that you did wrong to us?" "You yell and scream at us and embarrass us in front of our friends. Daddy argues with mommy and says mean things to her, but I never hear him confess anything!"

There was nothing wrong with the way the pastor was teaching from the pulpit! The problem was that his walk did not match his talk and the children saw the hypocrisy clearly.

Years ago, my children came home from school and were discussing a certain teacher no student liked. It seems this teacher demanded perfection in all the children but had no such expectation to change himself. Even little children see the hypocrisy and they react to it.

### Do you admit your own mistakes?

If your boss at work, your pastor, your teacher or your parent admitted their mistakes to you and asked for forgiveness for those things they did wrong to you, would you think more or less of them? The answer is more. Then why do we not admit our mistakes to the ones we are responsible to disciple? How else will our children, students, workers and church members learn?

It is time we began to be examples of a believer, and quit pretending to be a role model of God. Jesus is the only role model of God! *"The Son is the radiance of God's glory and the exact representation of His being,"* Hebrews 1:3. When we pretend to be a role model of God instead of an example of a believer, we are sinning.

### Are you willing to change yourself?

It is really hard to get our children to follow the Lord when we are following Satan. John and Mary went to church every Sunday. The rest of the week, they lived as the rest of the world — going to cinema, drinking, bad language — and were involved in some dishonest business practices. Now their children are into their teenage years and are getting more rebellious. In fact they do not want to go to church any longer and the parents come to you for advice. What would you tell the parents? Would you try to make them feel good (not their greatest need) by saying, "You are such good Christian parents, your child will come out of it soon" (a lie — the situation could get worse). Or would we say, "Your child just needs to sow some wild oats." (Do they?) "All children go through this stage." (Do they?)

Sad to say, this is a common problem. The parents are not as much puzzled as they are embarrassed. They know they have made mistakes and the rest of the world seeing those mistakes is downright embarrassing. God's wisdom deals with the problem directly. Parents must change their own lives FIRST! Parents and children BOTH have a sin problem! BOTH need to confess their past sins and then change and begin to live God's way. Parents CANNOT see clearly to take the speck of sin out of their children's life until they first take the log of sin out of their own (Matthew 7:5). This does not mean the parent must wait a long time before they can correct their child. But it does mean change must be evident in them and must be in process continually!

### Do your actions speak louder than your words?

Children at any age rebel when we expect that they change but we have no expectation to change ourselves. What God tells a Christian married woman in 1 Peter 3:1, concerning how to win over an unbelieving husband, is just as true for parents with a rebellious, unbelieving child. "*If any of them do not believe the Word, they can be won over without words by the behavior of their wives* (parents)." God says that you can win them over without speaking a word! How? By first dressing your self with a "*gentle and quiet spirit*," 1 Peter 3:4b. Any parent who demands that their child must change, but has no intention of changing their own life, is going to get more rebellion, not sainthood!

Suggest a more loving plan for the future. Encourage the good behavior and the steps the child is making to change and you will probably see more of it. Remember to keep working on your own life. God blesses faithfulness!

# Chapter 8

# Why is Discipline Needed?

### The battle is: Who is in charge?

The child WILL question your authority! Never forget that the child wants to be the one in charge in your house! If you let them, they will be. The child is playing the part of a fool every time they question your authority. Rise up to the challenge or your child will take on your rightful position of authority. By ten months or so, when the child begins to understand that "NO" means you are telling them to obey you, they will begin to test your sincerity. It is then that they will "give you the look" that says, "Do you really mean no?" This is the BIG TEST! IT IS ESSENTIAL THAT THE BATTLE IS FOUGHT CORRECTLY BY THE PARENT RIGHT HERE! You say "NO" to the child and if they continue in their foolishness, DON'T DISAPPOINT THEM! Paddle their backside. Remember they must feel some pain. *"You shall beat him with a rod, and deliver his soul from hell,"* Proverbs 23:13-14, NKJV. The word *"beat,"* is another word for spank. It does not mean beat them half to death. This is a command from God, not a suggestion. We do not want our children to go to hell. Very soon, the child will start to understand reasoning. But early on, they need to learn obedience. You should discipline especially when they are not listening to you. Do not shout!! Discipline on your part should be immediate, calm, completely without anger!

We discipline first of all because God tells us to! *"He who spares the rod hates his son, but he who loves him is careful to discipline him,"* Proverbs 13:24. Secondly, we discipline children because they belong to Him! God gives children to us on loan for a few years, but they are His children. In fact, God says, *"every living soul belongs to me,"* Ezekiel 18:4a. *"The earth is the Lord's, and everything in it, the world, and all who live in it,"* Psalm 24:1. It is a very serious offense to not bring up His/our children as the Lord tells us to.

153

We discipline children thirdly, because God tells us our children are sinful and corrupt, intent on doing evil. *"Folly is bound up in the heart of a child but the rod of correction will drive it far from him,"* Proverbs 22:15. A child may be born cute, but they are not born innocent. King David said, *"Surely I was sinful at birth, sinful from the time my mother conceived me,"* Psalm 51:5. In these verses, God shows us that our children are totally depraved, even at birth!

Fourth, Christian parents are to be a God-ordained tool by using corrective discipline to direct children towards heaven instead of hell. We can see this in the following verse. *"Do not withhold correction from a child, for if you beat him with a rod, he will not die. You shall beat him with a rod, and deliver his soul from hell,"* Proverbs 23:13-14, NKJV.

We can begin to see why Biblical discipline is a very loving act. We will realize that to withhold discipline is the world's way of living, not God's!

### Understanding God's discipline of us

God disciplines us because He loves us and wants to restore us. We will see that love and restore are key words. *"And you have forgotten that word of encouragement that addresses you as sons: 'My son, do not make light of the Lord's discipline, and do not lose heart when He rebukes you, because the Lord disciplines those He loves, and He punishes (scourges in NKJV) everyone He accepts as a son.' Endure hardship as discipline; God is treating you as sons. For what son is not disciplined by his father? If you are not disciplined (and everyone undergoes discipline), then you are illegitimate children and not true sons. Moreover, we have all had human fathers who disciplined us and we respected them for it. How much more should we submit to the Father of our spirits and live! Our fathers disciplined us for a little while as they thought best; but God disciplines us for our good that we may share in His holiness. No discipline seems pleasant at the time, but painful. Later on, however, it produces a harvest of righteousness and peace for those who have been trained by it,"* Hebrews 12:5-11.

We see that God disciplines us for our good, to develop righteousness and peace in us, and to restore us. Discipline from God may often be the fruit of His displeasure, but it is the proof of His love. God disciplines us, because like our children, we are spiritual beings who can and must learn right from wrong. We must discipline children for the same reasons that God disciplines us.

Discipline in the Bible is correction for the purpose of restoration and reconciliation. In the following paragraph from Hebrews, look carefully at how God uses discipline to heal us and love us.

We must especially know the difference between punishment and discipline, because many of the world's ideas are being practiced among Christians today, with the result being the destruction of families. Many well-meaning Christian parents have said that they would never spank their children due to some of the abuse (punishment) they have read about. But God, who especially knows the heart of a child, thinks a child should be spanked (Proverbs 13:24, 22:15, etc.) following certain rules. It is important to know that Biblical discipline is not punishment. Some day God will forever punish those who are not His children in the fires of hell. God's wrath will then be poured out. God's discipline of a believer then, is not retribution or vengeance but correction.

In the Bible, there are many good examples of how God disciplines instead of punishes. Even in one of the most difficult discipline situations, it is recorded in 1 Corinthians 5:5 that a man who was having sexual relations with his stepmother was put out of the church. This was not to punish him for his sins, but that *"his spirit may be saved in the day of the Lord."* God was interested in restoring this man and in this case even though Satan was allowed to destroy this body physically, his precious soul was saved for all eternity. Praise the Lord!

**But are not children of Christians born into the covenant?**

Yes, the children of believers, even of one believer (1 Corinthians 7:14), are born with a covenantal relationship with God. When a child is born into a true Christian covenant home, God sees a beloved child of His beloved child. Such a child then has the privilege/ advantage of hearing and seeing the gospel. God says there would be blessings for keeping covenant and curses for breaking it. Is this so in your home? Do the children see the gospel in your home?

## Is everyone a Christian parent?

A caution is greatly needed here. Not everyone who has a Christian name or attends a Christian church is a Christian parent. Christian parents are only those who see their sin as a capital offense against a holy and just God, believe the blood of Jesus Christ can save them, and are continually repenting of their sin (Mark 1:15). If a life is not CHANGED, it is not Christian! It needs to be said loudly that birth into a covenant family is not an automatic ticket to Heaven. In our churches around the world today, especially older mainline churches, there are many members whose parents and grandparents way back were Christians. So they think that they are Christian because of their family heritage, and because of the fact that they go to church every week. This is called "covenant presumption." But if their hearts are unchanged, they are covenant breakers and worse than pagans. A covenant breaker has heard the Word of God and has *"trampled the Son of God underfoot,"* or, not responded to the living or written Word (Hebrews 10:29-31).

## How did our children get corrupted?

A verse that shows how everyone became corrupt is: *"The Lord looks down from Heaven on the sons of men to see if there are any who understand, any who seek God. All have turned aside, they have together become corrupt; there is no one who does good, not even one,"* Psalm 14:2-3. In Romans 3:9-20 we see the same thoughts, *"There is no one righteous, not even one."* How did our kids and all of us become like this? Douglas Wilson in his book "Standing on the Promises" says:

"Children do not grow up to maturity and then decide whether or not they are going to be sinful by nature. Men and women do not come into this world morally neutral. Nor are we

156

basically good. By nature our entire race is in rebellion against God, and each of us is born into that rebellious race, inheriting the Adamic nature. This reality is not different for Christian homes – it is characteristic of all homes."

When Adam and Eve sinned long ago in the Garden of Eden, it was a sin that became part of the very nature of man, every man. Read more about it in Genesis 2 and 3. In the New Testament, we see that, *"Sin entered the world through one man, (Adam) and death through sin, and in this way death came to all men, because all sinned,"* Romans 5:12.

All are sinners and all die because Adam set the pattern for us. *"Through the disobedience of the one man, the many were made sinners,"* Romans 5:19b. In many places, the Bible talks about our "sinful nature" and "the natural man" showing that we were naturally born that way. Discipline has everything to do with this fact.

### Our children are born liars and cheaters.

A child is born "intent on doing evil and not good." We do not have to teach our children to lie, cheat, or steal. They do evil things naturally because they are self-centered. *"Even from birth the wicked go astray; from the womb they are wayward and speak lies,"* Psalm 58:3. We are naturally born loving self! We need to spend our time and energy by teaching children to deny self and do the right things. Biblical discipline will direct them and us to love God and others, and to hate sin and selfishness. All have to be taught that, and the sooner the better!

A selfish child who gets everything they want when they are young will get everything they want when they are older even if it is drinking, adultery, or other sinful habits. An angry child who is bossy and abusive becomes an angry adult who is bossy and abusive!

Discipline is the process God uses to turn a person from being selfish to giving, from wanting more to giving thanks for what they already have. Discipline is love!

**The little pagan boy next door did not corrupt your child.**

The world wrongly teaches that society or other people are the cause of all of our "bad nature" and if we can just change others, then all will be well.

God has a better idea. Discipline and teach the gospel. Teach the truth about who we are and our right responsibility to God and man from childhood. The real issue is: we all have wicked hearts that need to be turned to God and others. Only with this in mind will spanking a child make sense. But before we turn to the discipline of a child, God's rules for every home must be clear. How else would we know if a child broke a rule?

# Chapter 9

# When is Discipline Needed?

*"Folly is bound up in the heart of a child, but the rod of discipline will drive it far from him,"* **Psalm 22:15.**

Discipline is needed when the child is being a fool. Discipline drives out foolishness. But what exactly is a fool? We are foolish when we break God's laws. Why? Because anytime we break the laws of God we are saying our rules for living are more important. That is rebellion and foolish because we and our children will never get away with it. God disciplines all of us for breaking His righteous and holy laws. Spilling water or milk unintentionally is not foolish on the part of the child! That is an accident.

*"A fool's talk brings a rod to his back,"* **Proverbs 14:3a.**

If your child is mouthy and talks back to you and you do not discipline, you are creating a big problem for both you and for your child. The situation will continue to get worse not better if discipline is not used! Soon your child will disrespect all authority. Remember what the battle is! The child wants to be in control! If you let them be, they will most willingly take control, even at age one. Specifically when a child questions a parent's or God's authority, they are foolish and rebellious.

It will begin to happen something like this: A little baby will soon wail with a fake cry. A parent, especially a mom, knows the difference between a real cry and a fake one. They may just want to be held. The discipline for even a month old child is this: You do not need to rush and pick up a baby if nothing is wrong. It is okay if they cry a little. It won't hurt them. Just remember, a child is already selfish and they will most likely spin some kind of web to catch the parent to manipulate the parent very early in life. Expect it. Look for it.

## The first spanking

By the time a child is old enough to crawl and grab what they should not have, discipline must begin in more earnest. Say "NO," and slightly slap the child's hand when they reach for a glass they cannot have. Since they have never heard that "NO" word before, they will not understand right away. They will probably reach for it once more and we say "NO" again and slap their hand a little bit harder. At this point, the child may begin to cry but that is okay. Again they may reach for the object and we say "NO" and slap the hand still a little harder. This time they cry, but they are beginning to understand the "NO."

Of course it is wise to child-proof your home by putting your most valuable things out of reach. However, it may be a good idea to leave a plastic cup within the child's reach for an object lesson to teach "NO" and enforce obedience.

### *"A whip for the horse, a halter for the donkey, and a rod for the backs of fools,"* Proverbs 26:3.

As the child grows older and you say to them for their safety, "Do not cross this line that is too close by the road," watch for the child's response. They will MOST LIKELY go up to the line, step on it and look at you for your reaction. That little three-year-old is challenging you, thinking, "What are you going to do if I touch it or cross it?" "Do you really mean it?" Don't disappoint them! Here is where you need to win the battle! God has provided a soft spot on the butt of every child to be spanked. Don't use your hand; you may jar them with your broad hand or even hurt your hand. Sting their butt with a stick or wooden spoon. God says use a rod, implying a stick.

If you do not spank the child (and the child must feel some pain), the child will go further over the line. And if you still refuse to discipline the child, the child will in reality throw up their hands, shouting, "I am the boss," and you have a monster already. You then pass this child off to a teacher and wonder why the teacher can't handle the child.

Discipline is the parent's responsibility! The parent delegates that responsibility to the school when the child is there.

### Discipline while there is still hope!

*"Discipline your son, for in that there is hope; do not be a willing party to his death,"* Proverbs 19:18. God says we are a *"willing party"* to the death of our child if we do not discipline. We say we do not discipline because we love our children too much. God says we hate our children if we do not discipline them. God says, *"My ways are higher than your ways, and My thoughts than your thoughts,"* Isaiah 55:9b.

### Failing to discipline is sinful.

God always has the final word on what sin is. *"Anyone, then, who knows the good he ought to do (discipline) and does not do it, sins,"* James 4:17. *"Let the wicked forsake his way and the evil man his thoughts. Let him turn to the Lord, and He will have mercy on him, and to our God, for He will freely pardon,"* Isaiah 55:7. Praise God, He will forgive us and help us to do a better job, if we will just listen to His wisdom.

### Do your children know that they have broken God's rules?

The number one reason for all discipline is to direct us to honor and love God first, and others second. A parent must then primarily show how much God is hurt when we all sin! Is this fact not what forms a godly sorrow in us when we sin? Too often we sinfully point to our own authority instead of God's authority. Children need to know that the rules they break are God's rules. Specifically show the children from the book of Proverbs why they are in need of discipline. For example: If your boy has been fighting in school, show him God's wisdom of how *"a gentle answer turns away wrath, but a harsh word stirs up anger,"* Proverbs 15:1.

Children need to know that not only have they failed, but that they have failed God!

### What can I do? My child is now a rebellious teenager and I have not disciplined in a right way.

Have you failed to properly discipline from three years old to the teenage years and it has resulted in various kinds of rebellion? If you have, then you need to set the child down and explain exactly what you did wrong and what was the result of it. Explain how your permissiveness greatly tempted them to have a lack of respect for your authority and all authority. Explain how this will have even more serious results in their life in the future unless something changes. Explain you are very sorry for what that has done to them. Ask for their forgiveness! Now explain how things are going to be different. Make sure you establish the rules (God's rules) very carefully and carry through on doing things in a right way, even if you do not feel like it. Your child is not too old to discipline if he or she is still under your roof!

Perhaps spanking is difficult for a teenager who has never been spanked, but there are other effective ways to discipline. If you need water for your household every day, get a few extra empty jugs and have the teenager get the water. Even if you do not need it from your pump or tank let the child get it anyway. What other task are there in your household that need to be done? Do you need vegetables cut up? Do you need the floor swept or the dishes washed? In such a way, when the job is accomplished the discipline is over! Relationships can continue and it is important that they do. If we have not disciplined properly, our job will now be much harder whether we are in the home, business, school or church. However, God's rules still need to be obeyed.

### God's Ten Rules are for every home.

Even if we are 100 years old, God's children need to keep the commandments! Put up the Ten Commandments in the house. These are practical rules! Discipline is needed when these rules are broken.

## But how long do I spank my child?

It depends on the offense and the stubbornness of the child. Two to five hits is reasonable. But, better one hit and the child feels pain than ten where the child feels no pain. How long would you hit a horse or an ox that refused to be obedient? Twenty little hits with no pain would be scratching their backs for doing wrong. One hit with pain would begin to train! Some parents say, "NO" to the child and then grab them and hug them. A smack and some pain must be in between. *"A whip for the horse, a halter for the donkey, and a rod for the back of fools,"* Proverbs 26:3. With an animal, if you can control their head, you can control their direction. This is also true with children. Foolishness needs to be driven out of their head/heart, using a stick, with pain so they stop thinking like a fool.

Some kids will cry before you spank. Still you must spank! Early tears are usually false guilt trying to manipulate the parent to not discipline. Be wise to it, or you will build a Pharisee.

## Is "grounding" Biblical discipline?

The term grounding is used here as making a person stay home for two weeks, a month, or more, all as a form of discipline. "Grounding," is also being denied privileges for a length of time. The problem with grounding is that the discipline goes on and on for a length of time and is not, "over with." This is not an easy issue. But, think back at the problems and solutions we addressed already. Discipline should be immediate, confession should be made, forgiveness must be granted, and a reaffirmation of love must be established. These essential ingredients are mostly missing in grounding, especially the reaffirmation of love.

With grounding, the whole "aroma" of the house usually remains polluted. Why is this? Is it not that bitterness and resentment most often follow grounding, not peace and restoration? The parents suffer as much as the kids when discipline is extended over a period of time. I do not see evidence of God grounding anyone as a disciplinary measure.

In Exodus 22, God prescribed a fine or restitution, not grounding, as discipline for stealing or misusing someone's property. God's wisdom here teaches restoration and showing love for the one who was hurt.

### Are you consistent in applying discipline?

The certainty of discipline, not the severity of discipline corrects kids! Too often, we as parents let the little things go when the kids do wrong. Then as these little things build up, so does our frustration. Suddenly we unload on the poor kid and almost take their head off. The child/worker/student does not understand this kind of explosion. They do not see how you can add up all these little offenses and make one big offense out of it. You could not even train a dog, ox, or horse in such an inconsistent manner. Be consistent, under control, discuss the matter, discipline in love and share a little pain. Reaffirm your love and rejoice in the change!!! Don't forget to rejoice in the change!

# Chapter 10

# How to Discipline?

**Begin by encouraging your child to confess their sin.**
*"If we (a child also) confess our sin, He is faithful and just and will forgive us our sins and purify us from all unrighteousness,"* 1 John 1:9. Nothing is more important than confessing sin. The world hates the notion, but God sees it as humble submission to His will and as worship! 1 John 1: 6-10 show us the importance of confession to the restoration process. To fail to seek a confession of sin when discipline is needed is sin on the parents' part. For if a child has not sinned, they should not be disciplined. If they have, they should confess it. A Biblical confession humbles us before God and man! What better way is there to teach the gospel, God's hatred for sin, and His willingness to forgive?

**Do you forgive your children after you discipline them?**
God forgives us after we confess. Is there any better place to teach forgiveness and grace than when a child has done wrong and how God and the parent is willing to forgive them? But be careful here, it is not hypocritical to discipline a child you have forgiven. The reason is, discipline is a consequence of their sin and proof of your love for their soul. For example, a child steals from a store and gets caught. The child then confesses to God, to the parent and even to the storeowner, and they are forgiven by all. But, the child is still made to repay all that was taken as a consequence of the sin.

Not only must we forgive our children after we discipline them, we must let the children know that God forgives them also. This is IMPORTANT! God forgives our children and us when we confess our sins and He cleanses us from all unrighteousness, 1 John 1:9. Are we restored with our children after we discipline them, or do we sinfully hold a grudge of some kind? When we do, we not only fail to teach the gospel, we endanger our own forgiveness. *"For if you forgive men when they sin against you, your heavenly Father will also forgive you. But if you do not forgive men their sins, your Father will not forgive your sins,"* Matthew 6:14-15. Forgiveness is essential!

If your children are alienated from you and God after discipline, something is really wrong! Restoration is the goal of discipline. Both you and the children need to know it! Besides confession and forgiveness, there are some other serious issues that contribute to not being restored in a Biblical way.

### Do you discipline in anger?

Never discipline in anger! God doesn't! Hebrews teaches that God disciplines us because He loves us. The purpose of disciplining a child is correction for the purpose of restoration! Anger destroys. Love restores. God in His grace forgives and restores us! If we in anger carry on a big grudge, we will not be able to pull our children back into our arms as God does to us! Disciplining in anger is abuse. If you are angry, wait and pray first, unless the child is almost getting run over by some kind of motor vehicle.

We so often justify our anger as righteous. In James 1:20, God says our anger is *"not righteous!"* Who do you think is right? An example will help. Our child has just beaten a neighbor girl who is bruised and dirty from the beating. So we grab our child and almost pull their arm off, scream at them and throw them around because they hurt the neighbor girl. Our child who was just improperly disciplined begins to think, "It's not okay for me to get angry and fight. But is it okay for my mom/dad to get angry and fight me!" Anger in discipline is a good example of being right in what you do, but wrong in how you do it. Don't stop disciplining. Correct how you do it.

### "But how do I get my children to listen if I don't get angry?"

In response to this teaching, one woman said, "But my children will not listen to me until I shout at them with anger." "Exactly," I told her, "you trained them like that." The children know that you will not do anything to them when you are "under control." Tell them of your error in the past. Tell them that from now on you will say any request only once, softly, and then you will discipline, not so softly. You do not ever need to shout again! Some parents count to three before they discipline. That's not much better. One and two mean nothing. Three means it's time to get moving. Children need to learn to obey promptly and respectfully. Their life will be blessed if they do. Set the rules. Follow the rules. Explain the wrong. Discipline in love. If your discipline is a release of anger to make you feel better instead of correcting them, then you are very self-centered.

### Remember to reaffirm your love after you discipline!

After God disciplines us, He draws us close to Himself in a sweet embrace. Do we want and need God's tender hugs after we have done wrong? Yes, of course! Well, a child also needs the same thing from a parent. Like God teaches us, we must teach the child to hate the sin. And like God, we must take the repentant sinner into our arms and reaffirm our love. If we find it hard to reaffirm our love, it is probably because we disciplined in anger.

### Does pain really have to be involved in discipline?

Right after God gave us the commandments, He said there would be blessings for obedience and curses for disobedience. In fact, Deuteronomy 28 lists 14 verses of blessings and 54 verses of curses for disobedience. When it comes to curses for disobedience, plague, drought, defeat by enemies, people taking your possessions, body pain, hungry, thirsty, naked are all PAINFUL curses listed in Deuteronomy 28 for being disobedient. God even gave the Apostle Paul a painful thorn in the flesh to keep him humble. God never wastes pain. "No pain no gain" is a Biblical concept. Pain is a heavenly tool (pry bar) with eternal results.

### But I do not want my child to feel pain and cry!

How many times have you heard the above statement said, or said it yourself? If you think it is cruel or unloving to have your child feel pain in the discipline process, then listen to God who knows the heart of everyone better than we do! *"Do not withhold correction from a child, for if you beat him with a rod, he will not die. You shall beat him with a rod, and deliver his soul from hell,"* Proverbs 23:13-14, NKJV. It is not fun to hear our child cry today! But would it not be better to hear our child cry now, than to have them cry in the fires of hell for all eternity? If we refuse to discipline, we think lightly of our child's eternal soul! God said, *"Those I love I rebuke and discipline,"* Revelation 3:19a. Would you spank your child if you knew it was done for love and it would deliver their soul from hell?

### Do you discipline in private?

How would you like it if God told others about the lustful or evil thoughts you had? How would you like it if you said something wrong to someone in your family and they went all over the neighborhood telling everyone what you did wrong? You would rightly say, "A family does not act like this." Or, you would say, "Why did you not come and tell me alone?" Love goes alone to someone who has wronged you. *"Show him his fault, just between the two of you,"* Matthew 18:15b is always the first rule of Biblical discipline. Whether in business, the church, the school or the home, this is the most essential rule.

Fear-based rule disciplines in public and tries to get people to change through intimidation. Once again, this works, but not near as well as the loving way! If your boss, teacher, or pastor, went to your friend or associate in the workplace, church, or school and told of your mistakes but did not talk to you, you would surely be thinking, "Why did they not talk to me about it first?" This rule is just as true in the home! If we do this wrong, we *"provoke to anger,"* Ephesians 6:4, the very one we are commanded to disciple in love! May we see our personal faults, and change!

### Don't threaten or use harsh words instead of discipline.

It is very common for some parents to scream or threaten in the place of discipline. A father, employer, teacher or pastor who threatens with just words should know that, *"A servant cannot be corrected by mere words; though he understands, he will not respond,"* Proverbs 29:19. Stern words of instruction may be needed, but if it does not accompany discipline and pain, you will need to raise your voice more and more in the future. A person who has to raise their voice to try to gain control, is out of control.

### Are you teaching your child to submit to discipline?

Here is an issue that is especially critical. Sulking, pouting, or extended crying must not be allowed to continue long after discipline is administered. Why? Because pouting is self-centered behavior that is still demanding, "to have my own way." Pouting is bitterness, brooding, planning revenge, and is in general a proud spirit. Pouting is the opposite of submission and restoration – the main goals of discipline. In the early stages of the child's life, do not allow these temper tantrums and pouting by simply disciplining them more if they try it. Remember that obedience and submission needs to happen in a child even before they can understand why it is important for his or her future life. If you have to chase your child to discipline him, that is not submission! A child willingly bending over a chair to receive discipline is the right kind of attitude.

### Why is a lack of submission so wrong?

If your child does not learn to submit willingly to your rules in the home, how will they ever learn to submit to God's rules for all of life? Can you imagine a child of age 18 who never learned to submit? If they have not learned to submit to you and your rules, why should they listen to their new boss? And, what will they do when their new boss rebukes them and disciplines them? This is what they will do. They will follow their old pattern and be bitter, angry and most likely to cry and whine to many other people. How would you like such an employee? And then remember, the church and the school also have this same principle at work.

It is especially important for the parent to explain to the child as they are getting older of this necessity to submit. Here you have the opportunity to set one of the most important godly habits for the whole life of the child. If a child learns to submit calmly and respectfully to your discipline at an early age you will do much to protect him or her later in life! Can you see how you can begin to protect your child from anger, bitterness, fear and worry and much more by faithfully discipling as God instructs us to? Be assured this necessity to receive discipline starts by age one or before.

### How can we model submission?

*"Do not lose heart when He rebukes you,"* Hebrews 12:5b. Keep a good attitude when God disciplines you for your good! You can talk about how God is disciplining you personally for your mistakes. You do not have to be a grandparent before you will admit your mistakes to your children! Do it when you are a young parent so that your children can learn from your mistakes and how to submit. When we and our child willingly submit to God's discipline, we will live well in this life and enjoy an eternity together with God in the next! *"Submit to the Father of our spirits and live!"* Hebrews 12:9b.

### What will happen if I do not discipline?

It you still refuse to discipline, this is what God says will happen. *"He who ignores discipline comes to poverty and shame,"* Proverbs 13:18. It is not even financially wise to ignore the call to discipline. Do not forget God brings blessings for obedience. That includes financial blessings! How true this is in business also! *"The rod of correction imparts wisdom, but a child left to himself disgraces his mother,"* Proverbs 29:15. Letting a child do his or her own thing will be a *"disgrace,"* or lack of grace, to the family, business, church, or school.

### Dear child of God, it can be *"well with you"*!

*"Honor your father and your mother, as the Lord your God has commanded you, so that you may live long and it may go well with you,"* Deuteronomy 5:16a. *"Oh, that their hearts would be inclined to fear Me and keep all My commands always, so that it may go well with them and their children forever,"* Deuteronomy 5:29! God promises a blessing to parents and their children when the commands of God are kept. He will bless you also!